A

PASSION FOR

WELLNESS

A
PASSION FOR
WELLNESS

Healthy Employees,
Healthy Bottom Line

RACHEL A. SAPOZNIK

Published by Advantage, Charleston, South Carolina.
Member of Advantage Media Group.

ADVANTAGE is a registered trademark and the Advantage colophon is a trademark of Advantage Media Group, Inc.

Printed in the United States of America.

ISBN: 978-1-59932-614-6
LCCN: 2015954778

This publication is designed to provide accurate and authoritative information in regard to the subject matter covered. It is sold with the understanding that the publisher is not engaged in rendering legal, accounting, or other professional services. If legal advice or other expert assistance is required, the services of a competent professional person should be sought.

Advantage Media Group is proud to be a part of the Tree Neutral® program. Tree Neutral offsets the number of trees consumed in the production and printing of this book by taking proactive steps such as planting trees in direct proportion to the number of trees used to print books. To learn more about Tree Neutral, please visit **www.treeneutral.com**. To learn more about Advantage's commitment to being a responsible steward of the environment, please visit **www.advantagefamily.com/green**

Advantage Media Group is a publisher of business, self-improvement, and professional development books and online learning. We help entrepreneurs, business leaders, and professionals share their Stories, Passion, and Knowledge to help others Learn & Grow. Do you have a manuscript or book idea that you would like us to consider for publishing? Please visit **advantagefamily.com** or call **1.866.775.1696**.

To my parents who taught me
that good health is essential to a great life.

And for the health of our children and grandchildren who will
inherit this great nation, the United States of America.

TABLE OF CONTENTS

FOREWORD

In 2006, I had just become market president for a large national insurance provider. In my new role, I was tasked with growing the company's market share in the South Florida region.

The insurance provider often used brokers and agents to reach its customers, making those brokers and agents essentially the front-end sales force for our company. I've always believed that having a good relationship with the area's top sellers is very important for growing a business, so I asked my staff for the name of the best brokers in the region, and I was given the name of Sapoznik Insurance, a health and wellness insurance benefits agency. At the time, the firm was the top broker selling business insurance for small and midsize groups, as well as some larger groups.

To begin cultivating our relationship, I met with Rachel Sapoznik, the company's founder. Rachel appreciated that I wanted to talk to her and learn from her, and she was eager to provide input that would make our relationship stronger. She helped me understand that we needed to expand our product portfolio and become more nimble and price-competitive.

At the time, most insurance carriers were not focused on wellness. There was a medical department that looked at claims to ensure the services patients were receiving were appropriate and communicated with members about the different ways they could improve their health.

While wellness and prevention were fairly new concepts at the time, Rachel developed innovative plans and strategies to help companies like ours become more proactive. Our goal was to expand our products, offer competitive pricing, and focus on prevention and wellness in order to become a preferred health insurance supplier for Sapoznik's customers.

With her help, we were able to extend beyond our normal business practices by aggressively expanding various prevention measures for our customers. Rachel's input helped us develop additional insurance plans that were more appealing to business customers. We increased the number of products, or plans, that we made available to the market. We looked at the whole pricing structure of those products to make sure they were competitive, and we increased our level of service to customers, following the guidance that she provided.

Rachel's focus on wellness and prevention is appealing because everyone wins: our customers win because they're healthier, insurance carriers win because there are fewer claims, and Sapoznik Insurance wins because it builds and solidifies relationships with customers who rely on the company for future needs.

Today, our nation is experiencing out-of-control healthcare costs. Even with the Affordable Care Act now giving access to the uninsured through federal exchanges, costs continue to rise as a result of our unhealthy habits. One of the best ways to reduce spending on health-care is to control preventable diseases through improved diet and lifestyle. We can educate people about preventable diseases through wellness, prevention, and maintenance programs. First, individuals are made aware of risks to their health, then programs help them manage those risks so they can prevent or correct behaviors that lead to poor health. The result is less utilization of healthcare services, which reduces spending across the healthcare industry.

Because of their success, wellness and prevention programs are now becoming the centerpiece of the healthcare industry, not only for the insurance companies but also for physicians and healthcare organizations.

Rachel Sapoznik is one of my favorite people. I have tremendous respect for her business acumen, and I am continually inspired by her passion for helping businesses continue to thrive and succeed in our changing healthcare environment. I consider her a unique and highly respected individual in the industry, and I'm excited about the work she is doing to promote wellness and control healthcare costs.

George Foyo
Executive Vice President
Chief Administrative Officer
Baptist Health South Florida

ACKNOWLEDGMENTS

A Passion for Wellness is a journey that was not taken alone. I would like to express my sincere gratitude to all who supported and encouraged me throughout this process. There are so many people to thank for their contributions to my inspiration and knowledge and their help in creating this book. First, thank you to my family and friends for your patience as I took on yet another challenge – my sisters, Sarah Franco and Betty Goodman, my brother-in-law, Andrew Goodman, and my dear friends, Sandra Corcia, Griselle Farbish, Gracy Weberman, Brandon Kress and John Tolan. To my children, Jacqueline and Michael—your opinions on the book gave me a much-needed millennial perspective. I am particularly indebted to my son, Isaac, who was with me step-by-step in the creation of this book.

I have had the pleasure of working with some really great people, clients, and partners throughout my career, and I want them all to know how much I appreciate their patronage and support. I want to especially thank George Foyo for graciously writing the foreword to my book. I have the utmost respect and admiration for his leadership in our industry. I would also like to thank my Director of Corporate Wellness, Mario Junco, for all his work in compiling the information for the book and Beatriz Lucki, my Director of Marketing, for always keeping me in check with my out-of-the-box thoughts and ideas. Finally, to the entire Sapoznik Insurance team—any endeavor that I take on would not be possible without your hard work, dedication to the company, and support. To you, I will be eternally grateful.

To the many others not mentioned here, thank you for your love and encouragement.

INTRODUCTION

I t's time to take control of one of the largest line items in your business: employee benefits. You will accomplish this by progressively changing your mind-set and the culture of your organization to understand and value wellness. This book was written to educate you—the CEO and the leadership team—on how making a paradigm shift from *sick care* to *well care* will help increase your profit margins.

Prior to healthcare reform, many employers offered benefits on a voluntary basis as part of their strategy for attracting qualified candidates and retaining valuable employees. It was a choice many employers made, but it remained entirely at their discretion.

With the Affordable Care Act (ACA) ensuring access to healthcare, there is a growing feeling among Americans that they're "entitled" to healthcare—they feel that they have a right to be seen for care, regardless of the cost. Since healthcare reform has been integrated into the business world, there is now a mandate that most employers must provide coverage for employees. That mandate has a direct impact on the bottom line for nearly all employers.

The Employer Shared Responsibility provisions of the Internal Revenue Code, which were added to Code by the ACA, state that employers must comply and offer health insurance coverage:

> For 2015 and after, employers employing at least a certain number of employees (generally fifty full-time employees or a combination of full-time

and part-time employees that is equivalent to fifty full-time employees) will be subject to the Employer Shared Responsibility provisions under section 4980H of the Internal Revenue Code (added to the Code by the Affordable Care Act). As defined by the statute, a full-time employee is an individual employed on average at least thirty hours of service per week. An employer that meets the 50 full-time employee threshold is referred to as an applicable large employer.[1]

No matter how you spin it, there is a cost for healthcare, and few will feel it more than American business owners come 2016, when they will be forced to provide healthcare for their employees.

You can take control of these expenses through education, strategy, and implementation. As an employer, the key is to transform the way employees view their benefits; instead of viewing the benefits as healthcare insurance to cover any disease or condition, employees and your company as a whole must view healthcare as *well care*. The best way to control costs is to empower people to stay healthy.

The 2007 Milken Institute study "An Unhealthy America: The Economic Burden of Chronic Disease," reported that more than half of Americans were dealing with one or more chronic diseases that cost the nation $1.3 trillion to treat.[2] A 2014 update to the report found that the organization's forecasts underestimated the increase in costs in the ensuing years by more than $28 billion.[3] These unexpected costs are due to the increasing prevalence of chronic, preventable conditions among Americans.

Employers can change that number if they begin to understand that everyone in their organization—their employees and the people they touch everyday—can be part of the solution. As we educate our workforce and begin to change the mind-set that healthcare is an entitlement, that messaging goes beyond the workplace and makes its way into the home environment. Once there, it affects every member of the family—spouses, children, and other family members—and then disseminates into society to change the mind-set of others in the community. Establishing a culture of wellness in America today is going to change the future of our country, resulting in a healthier, happier workforce and a more profitable, sustainable company.[4]

My goal with this book is to help you understand how you, as a corporate leader, hold the keys to solving some of the most important problems facing healthcare. While everyone needs to be a part of changing the healthcare system, this book addresses how business leaders can be the most integral part of the solution: you can influence your employees' health insurance rates and impact your bottom line.

Merriam Webster defines passion as "a strong feeling of enthusiasm or excitement about doing something." I wrote this book, *A Passion for Wellness,* because I am enthusiastic about what you and I can do together to transform the way our nation thinks about healthcare. I want to help you and other business owners drive this change by taking the initiative to rein in healthcare costs now. By doing so, we can ensure that the businesses that make up this country remain healthy and profitable throughout this period of change. Together, we can create a healthier America.

1   https://www.irs.gov/Affordable-Care-Act/Employers/Questions-and-Answers-on-Employer-Shared-Responsibility-Provisions-Under-the-Affordable-Care-Act

2   Ross DeVol et al., "An Unhealthy America: The Economic Burden of Chronic Disease—Charting a New Course to Save Lives and Increase Productivity and Economic Growth," The Milken Institute, October 2007, http://assets1c.milkeninstitute.org/assets/Publication/ResearchReport/PDF/chronic_disease_report.pdf.

3   Anusuya Chatterjee et al., "Checkup Time: Chronic Disease and Wellness in America," The Milken Institute, January 2014, http://assets1b.milkeninstitute.org/assets/Publication/ResearchReport/PDF/Checkup-Time-Chronic-Disease-and-Wellness-in-America.pdf.

4   Patricia Schaefer, "The Hidden Costs of Presenteeism: Causes and Solutions," Business Know-How, accessed July 22, 2015, http://www.businessknowhow.com/manage/presenteeism.htm.

CHAPTER 1

A DIFFERENT VIEW OF HEALTHCARE

Today, we think of healthcare as dealing with medical problems; that conception is what has caused the reactive behavior that influences how we manage health concerns. People are thankful to have health insurance because they want to be covered in case of a medical situation.

"Healthcare policy" alludes to the idea that a person needs health insurance in case something bad happens to him or her—that healthcare is reactive. What we want to do is change that view so that people instead think of healthcare as preventive. We want to start changing the phraseology from *healthcare*, or connotatively "sick care," to *well care*.

It has been our experience that fewer than 30 percent of employees view their healthcare as well care. We have to turn those numbers upside down—we need that 30 percent to become 70 percent of people who view their benefit as well care. This is the only way you, as an employer, are going to manage or avoid chronic illness claims that could significantly impact the future of your business.

Ultimately, we want people to stay healthy and to stay in control of their bodies; we want them to be glad they have a "wellness policy" rather than healthcare coverage. We want people to be glad that the reason they go to their doctor is for a wellness visit, not to be seen for chronic health conditions or problems arising from poor health.

What we're really trying to do is change the way we look at the entire healthcare system in order to change behavior.

THE COST OF CARE

When we start looking at the cost of wellness versus the cost of healthcare or "sick care," we discover the potential for substantial cost savings.

Average Annual Health Insurance Premiums and
Worker Contributions for Family Coverage, 2003-2013

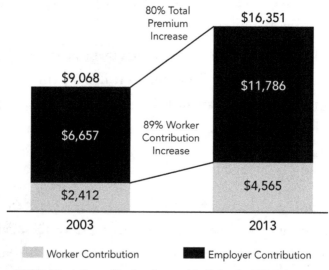

SOURCE: Kaiser/w Survey of Employer-Sponsored Health Benefits, 2003-2013

20

According to the Kaiser Family Foundation and Health Research & Educational Trust's "Employer Health Benefits 2013 Annual Survey," employers are paying nearly three-quarters of all premiums—$11,786 out of an average annual premium of $16,351.[1] What will happen to your bottom line if these costs grow?

Every time someone steps into an emergency room, it costs $2,500 to $3,000 to use his or her healthcare plan, according to a study funded by the National Institutes for Health, published in *PLOS ONE*, and reported on by *The Atlantic*.[2] These high costs can greatly affect future medical insurance renewals.

Had that person have gone in for a preventive, well care visit to avoid the emergency room, the cost would have been significantly less. That's because today, preventive screenings (which can lead to early detection of serious conditions leading to costly claims) are covered by most policies. These screenings including mammograms, and colonoscopies, and they typically are covered 100 percent under the preventative care provisions of health insurance plans. This is a far lower cost than that of undergoing treatment for more advanced forms of cancers that would have otherwise gone undetected and untreated.

Conversely, if people wait until they develop an adverse health condition, they could incur a bill that can easily surpass six figures. For example, if a man only finds out that he has high blood pressure after he has a heart attack or a stroke, the cost could be in the hundreds of thousands of dollars. But if he had known about his high blood pressure and been taking medication, eating right, and exercising, he could potentially have avoided that costly heart attack or stroke. The cost of medication is only a fraction of the cost of time in a hospital for treatment and a rehabilitation facility for his recovery.

We, as business leaders and employers, can rein in costs by understanding what we can do to educate our employees. We can control healthcare costs by having people understand how *they* do have control.

It is very important for each of us to shift the paradigm of employees perceiving benefits as an entitlement to one in which they take responsibility and proactively manage their healthcare. In the same way that an unhealthy society affects us all negatively, a healthy society affects everyone positively. If we don't shift our paradigm from entitlement to responsibility, then the future of healthcare may lead to a rationing of healthcare due to the exponentially rising costs.

As healthcare becomes more expensive and employers are faced with increases, something has to give. This is when businesses move into a reactive mode: What do you have to give up to manage your business's healthcare costs? How many people do you have to let go? How high do you have to make your deductible to pay for an increase in premium that affects everybody?

The truth is, only 20 percent of insured individuals are responsible for increasing costs, so 80 percent of us are being affected by the individuals who are not taking responsibility for their healthcare.[3] We're all affected by that person who decided that he didn't want to take control of his high blood pressure, didn't want to take his cholesterol medications or insulin, resulting in an emergency room visit.

We pay for anyone's lax attention to health; we pay for it in the form of increased premium costs and higher deductibles and by constantly having to change plans and carriers. We need to get everyone to understand that they need to be part of the process of achieving a healthy lifestyle because everyone is affected.

There are huge savings that come from being preventive and proactive versus being reactive when it comes to healthcare. As a business owner, you'll very quickly experience multiple effects when your employees view their benefits as a wellness plan rather than as a healthcare plan. Well care costs pennies on the dollar when compared to sick care benefits.

It's all about the paradigm shift. It's about getting your employees to view the benefits provided by your company as well care that is helping them stay healthy while reducing costs for both you (the employer) and the employee.

AN OUNCE OF PREVENTION IS WORTH MORE THAN A POUND OF CURE

Obese employees experience higher levels of absenteeism due to illness than normal weight employees. Normal-weight women miss an average of 3.4 days each year due to illness or injury. Overweight women miss 3.9 days, a 15% increase in missed days; obese women (BMI greater than 30) miss 5.2 days, a 53% increase in missed days; and women with a BMI of 40 or higher miss 8.2 days, a 141% increase in missed days, almost one week more of missed work each year than normal-weight women.

Normal-weight men miss an average of 3.0 days each year due to illness or injury. In comparison, overweight and obese men (BMI 25-35), miss approximately two more work days per year than normal-weight men, a 56% increase in missed days.[4]

Think about the cost of that missed work on a large employer. There are inordinate costs for temporarily replacing a person who is out sick, not to mention the slowdown of work and the redundancies that occur. According to the Gallup-Healthways study, the loss in productivity adds up to more than $153 billion annually in the United States.[5] That's very significant.

Obese workers file more workers' compensation claims, they have a seven times higher chance of having medical claims, and they lose thirteen times as many days of work because of injury.[6] Think about that as an employer. You're increasing your risk of workers' compensation claims because someone is not taking care of himself or herself.

According to Health Affairs (see chart below), the additional health costs associated with overweight employees is $170 for males and $496 for females. The problem isn't just medical, and it goes beyond health benefits costs and productivity slowdown—it can even affect work satisfaction.

Additional Health Cost of Overweight Employees

SOURCE: Health Affairs

Another costly and preventable illness affecting your business is the common flu. How disruptive is it to your team when you get that call from an employee who can't come to work because he or she has the flu? Or worse yet—if that employee comes in and contaminates the rest of the office? When employees come to work sick, they create an unhappy workplace, lower productivity, and may be distracted while at work due to their condition. All of this has a dollar value, which decreases profitability. This will be discussed in greater detail in subsequent chapters.

A healthy workplace is a more profitable workplace. When employers implement wellness programs, workers have fewer incidences of preventable and chronic diseases.[7]

ECONOMICS OF WELLNESS

Who's driving up healthcare costs? Statistically, we know that 5 percent of your employees are driving 50 percent of your total healthcare costs,[8] and between 70 and 80 percent of those healthcare costs are preventable or reversible, according to the CDC.[9] Sixty percent of employee absenteeism is related to psychological issues of job stress, according to the American Psychological Association.[10]

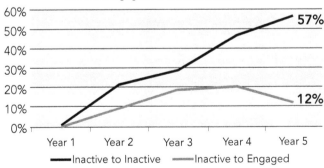

Longitudinal Study

Cumulative Trend for Initial Inactive Population That Became Engaged vs. Remained Inactive

45% cumulative trend reduction for members who became engaged

Average Medical Trend Over 5-year Period is 22% without Wellness Engagement versus 12% with Wellness Engagement

Actual results may vary
Source: Discovery Vitality Longitudinal Study of 374,479 members

When companies decide not to take an active role in their employees' healthcare—when they choose to be inactive and not participate in wellness—their healthcare claims over a five-year period increase by approximately 57 percent. This means that an employer must spend $1.57 on healthcare for every dollar it spent five years ago, an increase that far exceeds the rate of inflation.

If you think about not only those numbers but also the multiple effects of those numbers, then you will really feel the pain. For example, if you're spending $1 million in health insurance—which is normal for a company of about two hundred employees—then imagine having to spend 57 percent more for the same number of people five years from now.

If that same employer decides to go from a culture of inactivity to becoming engaged in healthcare through a wellness program, however, we have seen those healthcare costs increase by less than 13 percent over the same five year period. From an employer's perspective, the difference is significant.

A REVIEW OF WORKSITE WELLNESS PROGRAMS

A review of forty-two published studies of worksite wellness programs showed the following results:

- 28 percent average reduction in sick leave/absenteeism

- 26 percent average reduction in health costs

- 30 percent average reduction in workers' compensation and disability management claims costs

- $5.93:$1 average savings-to-cost ratio

A review of seventy-three published studies of worksite health-promotion programs showed an average $3.50:$1 savings-to-cost ratio in reduced absenteeism and health-care costs.[11]

Through our clients, we have seen employees benefit from receiving wellness education, prompting them to increase their participation company wellness initiatives including biometric screenings. Why is that important? Health conditions can only be prevented and reversed if there is early detection. If you don't know that you have high blood pressure, don't know that you're a diabetic, or don't know your body mass index (BMI), how are you going to manage your health? It's the unknown that costs millions of dollars. How does one place a monetary value on the heart attack or stroke that never happened or is waiting to happen?

We have cases where, in the third year of our program, 96.7 percent of the employees participated in biometric screenings. Participating in the screenings led them to increased engagement in disease management programs. This resulted in lower health costs through the management of chronic illnesses such as diabetes, high cholesterol, and obesity, the latter of which we know to be one of the fastest-growing illnesses today.

By encouraging employees to better manage their chronic illnesses, one employer reduced its claims by $2.5 million over a three-year period. The company, which was in the healthcare services industry, was approximately 17 percent below its peers in claims costs.

As a result of its reduced costs, the company was able to provide stability to its workforce and create a roadmap that enforced the idea that healthcare services should revolve around prevention and education. Ultimately, as we integrated healthcare wellness programs there, the company was able to use their healthcare savings as leverage for future acquisitions. For example, when the company began making acquisitions, it was able to submit a higher bid because it knew that when it brought a new entity into its program, it would be able to reduce the newly acquired property's healthcare costs.

SUCCESS RELIES ON BUY-IN FROM LEADERS

A very large automotive dealership, headquartered in southern Florida and with multiple dealerships through-out central Florida, started a relationship with Sapoznik Insurance when its leadership decided to implement a preventive education program to combat rising medical claims.

The majority of employees at the dealership were men between the ages of twenty-three and forty-five—auto technicians, service personnel, etc.—a group that we've found typically needs to be "nudged" a little to be proactive about its healthcare.

We brought health fairs to each of the dealerships. These fairs included biometric screenings for all team members. In addition to the health fairs, one of the programs we created was a unique, off-site event that promoted health and wellness through competitive sports and other challenges. The event was organized off-site to accommodate the large number of attendees.

In a local park, we organized competitions and challenges involving kayaking, mountain biking, tug-of-war, and other team-based activities. Our goal was to capitalize on the competitive spirit among the employees and to make them feel like they were a part of something greater. We also offered a variety of nutritious lunch options: water, veggie wraps, fruit, and other healthy choices.

Since we know that medical claims are also affected by dependents on an employee's plan, we opened up the event to spouses and children to spread the message of health and wellness to families.

As part of leadership's buy-in of the program, we had the owner take part in some of the events, which really resonated with the employees. It was something special to see the CEO kayaking through the mangroves and biking alongside other employees.

We've seen a strong correlation between leadership buy-in and the success of our programs, because employees become more motivated with the idea of wellness in the workplace when they see their executives participating. When employees feel they have buy-in from leadership, they are more motivated to take time out of a work day to take part in a biometric screening or other wellness activity.

The sporting event has since become an annual activity for the dealership. We've also implemented programs such as challenges between dealerships and using pedometers to measure the number of steps participants take and the number of miles they walk.

Another organization that sees the economic impact of corporate wellness, PepsiCo, was also able to save $3.78 in healthcare costs for every $1 invested in employee wellness programs.[12]

By creating a healthier work environment, we're able to redirect dollars that normally would have gone toward medical claims to fund growth and expansion. An example of this is when a private equity company is looking for acquisitions: having an effective wellness program that drives down claims costs can help it in the buying process. Since the company's leaders know that they can save money on premiums, they can use that money to outbid their competitors when purchasing a new company.

REDUCING ABSENTEEISM

One of the ways a wellness program benefits employers is by reducing absenteeism. Businesses can reduce absenteeism in the workplace by using some aspects of the preventive wellness programs. Companies that implement wellness programs have about a 28 percent reduction in sick leave.[13] No matter the size of the company, that percentage is significant in terms of productivity.

Using modern technology, we're able to introduce some very innovative program features. For instance, we are now introducing companies to the idea of telehealth through Virtual Health USA. The concept of telehealth has been around since the mid-1960s, but it has only recently come into its own as technology and regulations have made it more accessible to all consumers. Telehealth was first conceived as a way to provide healthcare services to underserved rural areas. It was strictly a doctor-to-doctor or doctor-to-nurse consultation, by either phone or dedicated video connection.

Today, telehealth is most often deployed over a smartphone, tablet, or laptop, and it is a telecommunications capability that allows employees to consult with a physician via two-way video, text, or e-mail. Many medical experts say that employees can receive some of the care they need from the comfort of their home or office. More than thirty-six million Americans have used telehealth in some way, and as many as 70 percent of doctor visits can be handled over the phone, according to a recent study by the Affiliated Workers Association, a network of professionals dedicated to empowering everyday employees.[14]

The convenience of seeing a licensed physician when and where you need it is a key selling feature of telehealth today. By using an online consult, the employee avoids a great deal of lost time—waiting days to see a physician, traveling to and from an appointment, waiting for the physician, waiting to check out at the end of the office consult, and then waiting at the pharmacy for any prescriptions. While the conveniences of telehealth are nice bonuses, it has also improved access to care, which should translate into avoided complications and improved overall health. This benefits everyone: the employer sees less absenteeism, the employee is more productive at work, and the physician is compensated for his or her online consultation.

While there is a great deal of focus today on using telehealth to treat minor illnesses and injuries, there is far greater potential for telehealth to increase access to second opinions, to more easily obtain lab test results and their interpretation, and for patient management pre- and postoperatively. It is also possible to obtain mental health services via telehealth, along with disease management and other services.

Employers and employees are just seeing the tip of the iceberg in telehealth. There will be many more advances in telehealth as providers incorporate mobile health devices and expand healthcare services beyond common health ailments.

Businesses that rely on every employee to perform critical tasks find themselves in a bind when absenteeism rises. As a business owner, you need to pay attention to the employees that abuse the time-off benefits you offer, and you should understand the effects of absenteeism on the bottom line.

In his article "The Effects of Workplace Wellness Programs on Absenteeism," Sam Ashe-Edmunds of Demand Media offers this data:

> When employees come to work ill or have ailing family members, they may work slower, cause more accidents or stop work to deal with family problems. A new mother, for example, may spend time on the phone with the family physician, be distracted from her work or have to leave for a doctor's appointment if

her child is ill. Employees who come to work feeling ill, have a negative impact at the office and are generally less productive. Offering healthy snacks, such as fresh fruit and juices, can help employees ward off a cold or flu ... The fewer sick and injured employees you have filing insurance claims, the lower your health-care costs, including insurance premiums. After the Lincoln Plating Company of Lincoln, Nebraska, insti-tuted a wellness program that included a prework stretching routine, work-related injuries among its employees declined 50 percent and workers' comp costs decreased by approximately $800,000. Union Pacific Railroad decreased employee healthcare costs 17 percent during the first five years of its employee wellness program, saving an estimated $1.26 million during its first year.[15]

Every fall, and as we head toward winter, we hear in the news that it's flu season. What does that mean to you, as an employer? A 2011 study conducted by Staples Advantage, the business-to-busi-ness arm of the office retailer, found that more than 35 percent of office employees cleaned their inboxes at least once a day, but only 15 percent of the workers clean their workspace once a week or more. The result, according to the International Sanitary Supply Asso-ciation, is 7.7 sick days per employee every year, which, the CDC reports, is costing $225.8 billion per year in lost productivity.[16]

According to Staples's fifth annual Flu Season Surveys, 60 percent of workers say they come to work with the flu.[17] This can be prevented simply by raising awareness about cleanliness—a study by the University of Arizona found that a person's desk has four hundred times more bacteria than a toilet seat.[18] It's all about going back to the basics: preventing the spread of germs by maintaining a tidy, clean desk, washing hands with soap and hot water for at least twenty seconds, and making sure you get your flu shot (which, according to experts, is the best way to prevent the flu).

It is up to employers to help create a different view of healthcare that will initiate the cultural shift in the health behaviors of their employees. Let's begin our journey.

1   "Employer Health Benefits 2013 Annual Survey," The Kaiser Family Foundation and Health Research & Educational Trust, accessed July 22, 2015, https://kaiserfamilyfoundation.files.wordpress.com/2013/08/8465-employer-health-benefits-20132.pdf.

2   Lindsay Abrams, "How Much Does It Cost to Go to the ER?" The Atlantic, February 28, 2013, http://www.theatlantic.com/health/archive/2013/02/how-much-does-it-cost-to-go-to-the-er/273599/.

3   Kullgren, "Does 20% of the population really use 80% of healthcare dollars?"

4   http://www.cdc.gov/workplacehealthpromotion/businesscase/benefits/productivity.html

5   Ibid.

6   Roberto Ceniceros, "Obesity Problems Weigh on Workers' Comp," Workforce Magazine, March 8, 2012, http://www.workforce.com/articles/obesity-problems-weigh-on-workers-comp.

7   "Give Productivity a Shot in the Arm: How Influenza Immunization Can Enhance Your Bottom Line," Partnership for Prevention, accessed July 22, 2015, http://www.prevent.org/data/files/topics/flu%20booklet_final.pdf.

8   Kullgren, "Does 20% of the population really use 80% of healthcare dollars?"

9   "The Power of Prevention," National Center for Chronic Disease Prevention and Health Promotion, 2009, http://www.cdc.gov/chronicdisease/pdf/2009-Power-of-Prevention.pdf.

10 Mary Corbitt Clark, "The Cost of Job Stress," Mediate.com, July 2005, http://www.mediate.com/mobile/article.cfm?id=1762.

11 Jeff Fermin, "10 Insane Facts About Corporate Wellness," Officevibe, October 21, 2014, https://www.officevibe.com/blog/infographic-corporate-wellness.

12 "Workplace Wellness Programs Can Cut Chronic Illness Costs; Savings for Lifestyle Improvements Are Smaller," Rand Corporation, January 6, 2014, http://www.rand.org/news/press/2014/01/06/index1.html.

13 Fermin, "10 Insane Facts About Corporate Wellness."

14 Jessica Harper, "Pros and Cons of Telehealth for Today's Workers," US News & World Report, July 24, 2012, http://health.usnews.com/health-news/articles/2012/07/24/pros-and-cons-of-Telehealth-for-todays-workers.

15 Sam Ashe-Edmunds, "The Effects of Workplace Wellness Programs on Absenteeism," Demand Media, accessed March 25, 2015, http://smallbusiness.chron.com/effects-workplace-wellness-programs-absenteeism-44347.html.

16 Lizzie Parry, "Why It's Time to Detox Your Desk: Average Worker Comes into Contact with More than 10 Million Disease-Causing Bacteria Lurking on Their Keyboard, Phone and Mouse," December 5, 2014, http://www.dailymail.co.uk/health/article-2859334/Why-s-time-detox-desk-Average-worker-comes-contact-10-MILLION-disease-causing-bacteria-lurking-keyboard-phone-mouse.html.

17 Shweta Agarwal, "Despite Drop in Number of Employees Going to Work Sick, 60 Percent Still Show Up with the Flu," Staples, October 15, 2014, http://investor.staples.com/phoenix.zhtml?c=96244&p=irol-newsArticle&ID=1977806.

18 "Survey Finds Desktop Dining Poses Food Poisoning Risk," Infection Control Today, August 23, 2011, http://www.infectioncontroltoday.com/news/2011/08/survey-finds-desktop-dining-poses-food-poisoning-risk.aspx.

CHAPTER 2

A HEALTHY WORKPLACE, A HEALTHY BOTTOM LINE

N ow that you are beginning to have a different view of healthcare, let me start by painting a picture of what a healthy company looks like. In my experience, the health of a company starts at the top, with an owner, a CEO, and a leadership team that really understand how important their employees are to their financial success.

A company's financial success really comes from having employees who are invested in the company vision, and for a long time, we haven't really considered employees' personal health as part of that equation. We've looked at what employees' actions were at work, but we haven't thought about how their personal health affects their contribution to the success of a business.

By focusing on wellness, what we're really trying to do is create a paradigm shift in the way that executives look at benefits—particularly now that we have fully implemented healthcare reform. The ACA is here to stay, and business owners, leadership, and public and private entities all need to understand how important healthcare is to the overall profitability of any institution or company, whether small or large.

What that paradigm shift looks like is a cooperative effort, starting from the top, with a clear understanding that we are all part of a solution—as opposed to being a part of a problem. When I say that, I mean that healthcare is becoming the largest expense—other than payroll—that any company has. But we can get a handle on healthcare costs, and that starts with executive leadership and education.

A SOLUTION THROUGH EDUCATION

Education starts with employees understanding that they can be part of the solution to the high cost of healthcare. They can do this by understanding the importance of taking care of themselves and then taking measures to change unhealthy habits.

People spend most of their waking hours at work; that's why work is the perfect platform for getting employees to really understand the crucial role they play in being part of the solution to a strained healthcare system.

It's important for employees to understand that chronic diseases such as hypertension (high blood pressure), diabetes, high cholesterol, and obesity account for $3 of every $4 spent on healthcare.[1] With education and a little effort, these illnesses are entirely preventable, and it's through education that we're trying to get people to understand that they have the power to keep themselves healthy.

We're not saying that people are not going to get sick or that they're not going to have issues with their weight, high blood pressure, or cholesterol. What we're saying is that if people have these conditions, then we want to help them understand how to control the problem so that they don't end up in the emergency room. Through education, we are preventing escalated medical conditions.

For example, if people are taking blood pressure medications, let's make sure that they take them as prescribed so that they don't become victims of a heart attack or stroke. Or, if they don't know that they have high blood pressure, let's find out so that we can get them on medication.

The cost of medication to manage a condition far outweighs the astronomical expense of going to an emergency room or hospital because of something that was preventable. The solution begins with education in the workplace.

The company truly needs to care about its people and employees, who in turn will care about where they work—absenteeism will go down, the number of workers' compensation claims will drop, there will be a reduction in healthcare claims, and as a result, productivity and profitability will increase. In other words, employers can show employees how much they care about them by implementing programs to help them stay healthy. By helping employees stay healthy, their emotional ties to your company become more entrenched. According to the *Principal Financial Well-Being Index*, employees say that employer-sponsored wellness programs encourage them to work harder, perform better, and miss fewer days of work.[2]

What does that mean for the company's owner and its leadership team? A healthier workforce has a significant impact on the company's profitability, resulting in higher margins.

"We care about your health," is the message that resonates loudly with all age groups in the workforce today. Educating employees about their health shows them that they are working for a company that looks at them as part of a team. Not only are you building a much stronger team when employees feel that you care about them, but they're going to return the sentiment by going the extra mile.

When employees feel that they're working for a company that cares about their health, their employment is not just about money anymore; it's about working for a company that they want to be a part of their everyday lives. They no longer look at the company or their job as just a means for generating paychecks; they look at the workplace as part of a healthy lifestyle that continues even when they go home.

As employees become more educated, they share their knowledge with their children, their spouses, and their friends. That education has far-reaching implications that will help society at large address the critical issue of healthcare.

THE POWER OF CHOICE

As a place to promote the concept of wellness, the work environment is crucial to the evolution of the idea of healthcare. At a psychological level, people desire a sense of control, so by giving employees healthy choices, they feel in control and empowered, which benefits them and the company.

When we promote wellness in the workplace, we do so by bringing a full array of services to the employees. For example, the education piece is composed of various means of access to information because some people are visual learners and others are auditory learners. We also use consistent messaging, through components such as brightly colored informational posters and better vending machine options, to encourage people to make better choices. Through activities like a lunch-and-learn series, lunchtime fitness classes, audio programs, podcasts, and videos, we work with employees to influence them to adopt healthier eating habits and find ways to move more while at work. Our goal is to see employees succeed, and as they begin to adopt an attitude of wellness, their companies succeed in controlling healthcare costs.

STABLE HEALTHCARE COSTS

Employers that are not implementing a corporate wellness program are seeing their healthcare costs skyrocket.[3] Let's face it: What is more important to any person than their health? Unfortunately, most people don't really place enough emphasis on their health until it goes awry; once that happens, they start to realize how important good health is for their long-term well-being.

It's painful for employees to deal with health insurance issues such as changing carriers, making coinsurance payments, or budgeting for higher deductibles. But in educating employees, our goal is— with their help and cooperation—to mitigate unhealthy and costly behaviors or consequences. For example, we want employees to understand that they can avoid costly emergency room visits simply by taking their medications as prescribed.

When employees understand how important it is to be compliant, then they are able to help stabilize healthcare plans. The result? Employees are able to stay with their same carriers and doctors, and they're able to maintain copayments that are affordable. Having a stable healthcare plan that employees can afford for themselves and their families makes you, as an employer, even more valuable to them—this is a strategy in retaining high-performing employees and reducing turnover.

Every business wants to be profitable. To be ahead of the curve in business, companies need to be proactive in the face of changing dynamics. It's the same with healthcare. To avoid high claims and keep costs in check, business leaders need to look at healthcare from a different perspective. As an employer, you can be part of the solution by leading the charge to help employees understand how to be proactive—not reactive—about their health.

What does reactive healthcare look like? It looks like an emergency room visit that costs thousands of dollars. It looks like a heart attack or stroke that could have been avoided, or a tumor that could have been detected earlier. It looks like having to change your company healthcare plan because you can't afford it anymore. It looks like higher deductibles, higher copayments, and higher out-of-pocket costs because you did not take the proper steps to be proactive and get ahead of the curve.

Just think about this: What if you ran your entire company this way? How long will you be in business if you're constantly operating in a reactive mode? It's the same with healthcare—how long will you be able to battle the blaze of higher healthcare costs if all you're doing is putting out the fires of high claims? Why not prevent the fires in the first place by educating employees on wellness?

REAPING THE BENEFITS

Like anything worthwhile, obtaining a positive outcome takes an investment of time and other resources. What we've found is that those companies that are willing to take the time to invest in wellness for their employees are reaping the benefits. Those benefits include a total return on investment (ROI) of approximately $6 for every dollar that is spent on wellness.[4]

The total ROI an employer will capitalize on can be broken up into two parts.

The first is through healthcare costs because claims costs can be greatly reduced when you have a workforce fully engaged in a program that includes education, incentives, and on-site metrics and guidance. According to the 2010 study "Workplace Wellness Program Can Generate Savings" conducted by three Harvard researchers, this portion of the overall return equates to $3.27 for every dollar spent on a wellness program.[5]

The second part is through reduced absenteeism and workers' compensation claims. According to the Harvard study, an employer can experience $2.73 in savings for the costs of absenteeism for every dollar spent.[6] This combination of savings due to reduced healthcare claims, less absenteeism and fewer workers' compensation claims equals the total ROI of $6 for every dollar spent on wellness.

When your company has an organized wellness program that is fully endorsed by its top-level executives, the ROI on wellness trickles down into other areas of the organization including the every day lives of the employees. Wellness in the workplace is a holistic way to influence employees while they are at work and beyond, allowing them to become part of the solution not only at work, but also at home.

Wellness and healthcare don't just happen overnight; in our experience, it takes approximately three years to implement a viable wellness program strategy and achieve optimum outcomes. Implementing a wellness program is just like other initiatives in your business—there has to be a prescribed plan and process, which in this case includes building blocks to wellness.

The first of these building blocks is helping employees know their numbers. It's that simple: know and understand your numbers. It's amazing how many people really have no idea what their numbers are. We start out by educating people about knowing their blood pressure number, their cholesterol number, their BMI number, and how those numbers reflect their overall health.

What we find is that most people, even those who know their numbers, don't know what their numbers mean. Early in our program, we bring in nurses for biometric screening, and as part of that testing, it's very common for an employee to suddenly find out he or she has a problem. That fifteen- to twenty-minute assessment is often the first step in a lifelong journey to better health for that employee. We then focus on how people can keep their numbers in a normal range. For instance, few people take advantage of their wellness checkups, even though those visits to the doctor are now covered under most insurers' menu of preventive care services at no cost.

After we educate people on their numbers, we begin to build upon that knowledge by offering incentive programs for employees to participate in. We work to increase participation by creating achievement levels that allow employees to connect rewards to their progress toward achieving healthy activities and improving their numbers. While there are no penalties for nonparticipation, there are definite rewards for those employees who decide to become active and take advantage of preventive doctor visits. We'll discuss the power of incentivizing your employees through a corporate wellness program in greater detail in chapter 5.

PARTICIPATION BREEDS LOYALTY

Part of the challenge of deploying a wellness program at work is helping employees overcome their suspicions about motive. Our goal is to ensure that employees understand that everything measured is protected by the Health Insurance Portability and Accountability Act (HIPAA)—employers do not have access to any employee's personal health information. After an assessment, only the employee knows what health issues he or she has.

It's also important to understand that this is not some "Big Brother" initiative. We're trying to educate employees about how the things they're doing impact their lives, the entire company, and that of their family outside the workplace. Our goal is to make employees want to change their own behavior.

In addition to stabilizing healthcare costs, another benefit of a wellness program is the stabilization of the workforce; a wellness program improves employee retention. Turnover is very costly for an organization, regardless of size. It has been our experience that people who participate in employer-sponsored wellness programs tend to stay employed by that company longer.

A comprehensive wellness program doesn't just stabilize healthcare costs; it ensures that you have happy, healthy, productive people in the office every day, which improves the health of your bottom line. A wellness program helps create not only a financially healthy workplace, but also a healthy place to work.

THE NEW WORLD OF HEALTHCARE

As discussed previously, with the enactment of the ACA, we're seeing a new world in healthcare. According to the Heritage Foundation's report, "Federal Spending by the Numbers, 2014," today, 25 percent of every dollar spent goes toward healthcare.[7] American healthcare is a $3 trillion industry, and now the ACA is forcing even more people, many of whom have never had health insurance or have accessed the healthcare system before and may have major medical issues, into an already strained system.[8]

Where Did Your Tax Dollar Go?

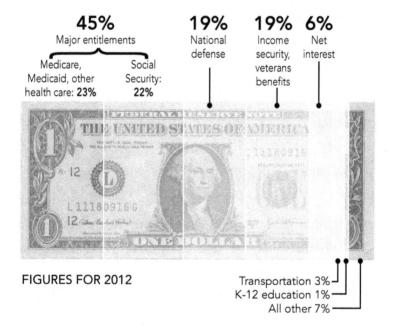

45%
Major entitlements

Medicare, Medicaid, other health care: **23%**   Social Security: **22%**

19%
National defense

19%
Income security, veterans benefits

6%
Net interest

FIGURES FOR 2012

Transportation 3%
K-12 education 1%
All other 7%

Notes: Income security includes federal employee retirement and disability, unemployment compensation, food and housing assistance, and other federal income security programs. Figures have been rounded. National defense includes overseas contingency operations.
Source: Office of Management and Budget, *Historical tables: Budget of the U.S. Government, FY 2014*, Table 8.4, April 2013, http://www.whitehouse.gov/omb/budget/Historicals (accesssed May 8, 2013).

Federal Spending by the Numbers 2013. heritage.org

The ACA has many people feeling that healthcare is an entitlement. Experience shows us that when people feel they are entitled to something, there's no personal accountability; this inevitably leads to excess, redundancies, and wasted spending in our healthcare system.

Furthermore, the ACA is going to force employers to pay for healthcare. Employers who don't address the situation are going to face difficult decisions when it comes to growing their businesses.

If your business has waste, it's because you're spending dollars on things that are not necessary. There's only one way to spend a dollar, and once that dollar is spent, you don't have it to spend on other areas of the business. You may have to give up hiring more employees. You may have to give up that new building you needed in order to expand or hold off on the new equipment you needed to buy. All of the things that your business may need, might have to be sacrificed because no consideration was given to controlling the costs of healthcare.

Therefore, it is incumbent upon employers to understand that if they don't get a handle on their healthcare costs, they're going to lose money. That loss is going to impact every facet of the business, including pay increases, development, and growth.

The cost of benefits plans will skyrocket as previously uninsured employees enter the insurance pool. These employees may not understand that they can be part of the solution to controlling your company's costs, or they may have no idea how to participate in your company's efforts on that front. This doesn't need to be the situation because the truth is that no one's really brought it to employees' attention that they can be part of the solution.

Again, chronic diseases are the main cause of increasing healthcare costs. But chronic diseases are controllable and manageable. Chronic diseases cost pennies on the dollar if they are held in check. This will be discussed further in chapter 3.

There's also going to be a push when it comes to managing claims; we are certainly looking at reaching a place where patients are not going to have access to all the doctors that they want, because the system simply can't afford to allow it. Hospitals are not going to be able to provide services that we would like them to because they're so overwhelmed due to all the additional patients being seen. Even people with insurance are not going to be able to get care when they need it; they won't be able to get in to see a doctor because there are too many patients and not enough physicians.

Right now, if you had to have open heart surgery or a hip or knee replacement within a week, you could probably have any one of those services. But for less-urgent conditions, the waiting lines are already starting to build in America. If you look at what's going on in Canada, England, or France, it sometimes takes months before a patient is able to get services, which is something Americans are not used to.[9]

BENEFITS TO EMPLOYERS

Employers are always looking for ways to increase margins without increasing costs or hiring more people. The way to achieve this is by building a healthier, more productive workforce.

With some up-front effort and an organized strategy, an employer can start pushing its healthcare costs back down or, at the very least, take real strides to stabilize them. For instance, one of our clients saved $1 million in claims in 2014 as a result of preventive visits to the doctor. Why? Because those doctor visits helped address the management of chronic diseases and avoid costly emergency room visits.

As the company saw an increase in education, which resulted in more preventive medical visits, its claims costs went down by $1 million. In addition to the education component, another area that drove this incredible change was the buy-in from ownership and the leadership team. As an employee, it is extremely powerful to have your CEO stand beside you in solidarity as you push ahead toward better health. It's one thing to have received a motivational memo from your CEO, but it's even more encouraging when you are side-by-side with your CEO during an employer sponsored 5K.

This type of "do as I do, not just as I say" approach is in many ways the "X-Factor" companies need in order to spark change. When leadership is involved, the trickle-down effect touches managers, supervisors, and staff. That's when real change occurs because the notion of corporate wellness moves from being a company initiative to being an actual part of the culture. With this type of involvement, biometric screenings are even better attended, resulting in greater predictive modeling of chronic diseases within the organization.

Saving $1 million in claims does not happen by accident; it is the result of a well-rounded approach to wellness and a commitment to incremental behavioral change. These changes begin with the support of leadership and are encouraged through incentives and smart premium-contribution strategies that transform companies from organizations that provide reactive healthcare to ones that promote proactive well care.

So what did the company do with that $1 million? It used the money to expand its business, open a new facility, and hire new employees. The pendulum could have swung the other way; the company could have, instead, spent $1 million *more* in claims, forcing it to reduce its workforce. Its margins would have been down, and opening a new facility would have never been possible—in fact, they may have had to close a facility.

As significant as that $1 million savings was—and it was realized in a short period of time—companies that initiate and consistently maintain wellness for many years see even more dramatic savings and outcomes.

For example, since 1995, the percentage of Johnson & Johnson employees who smoke has dropped by more than two-thirds. The number of employees who have high blood pressure or are physically inactive has also declined by more than half. This is great news, but should it matter to managers? It turns out that a comprehensive, strategically designed investment in employees' social, mental, and physical health has certainly paid off. Johnson & Johnson's leaders estimate that wellness programs have cumulatively saved the company $250 million on healthcare costs over the past decade.[10]

Wellness programs have often been viewed as a nice extra rather than as a strategic imperative. Newer evidence tells a different story. With tax incentives and grants available under recent federal healthcare legislation, American companies can use wellness programs to chip away at their enormous healthcare costs, which are only rising with an aging workforce.

Employers need to look at healthcare through a new lens. Most CEOs today just look at health benefits as a line item of cost when they should be viewing it more as a line item that can drive increased profits.

It's time for employers to change their mind-set about the healthcare benefits they offer employees. It's time to be engaged in the wellness side of healthcare; that's the only way to change behavior and make healthcare positively impact your bottom line.

We want employees who feel a sense of responsibility, who are engaged, and who take responsibility for their work and their health. We want employees who want to become our partners in moving the company forward.

Employers will begin to see some near-immediate results—increased productivity, better attitudes, and lower turnover—because employees realize right away that they're working for an organization that cares about them. The time to get started with the process is now so that you can reap the rewards of what wellness can do for your employees and your business.

1   The Impact of Chronic Diseases on Healthcare," Triple Solution for a Healthier America, 2015, http://www.forahealthieramerica.com/ds/impact-of-chronic-disease.html..

2   Stephen Miller, "Wellness Programs as an Employee Retention Tool," Society for Human Resource Management, January 20, 2010, http://www.shrm.org/hrdisciplines/benefits/articles/pages/wellness_employeeretention.aspx.

3   Leonard Berry, Ann Mirabito, and William Baun, "What's the Hard Return on Employee Wellness Programs?" *Harvard Business Review*, December 2010, https://hbr.org/2010/12/whats-the-hard-return-on-employee-wellness-programs.

4   Ibid.

5   Katherine Baicker, David Cutler, and Zirui Song, "Workplace Wellness Programs Can Generate Savings," Health Affairs, *Health Affairs* 29, no. 2 (February 2010), doi:10.1377/hlthaff.2009.0626, http://www.workplacewellness.com/images/Workplace_Wellness_Programs_can_generate_savings.pdf.

6   Ibid.

7   Romina Boccia, "Federal Spending by the Numbers, 2014: Government Spending Trends in Graphics, Tables, and Key Points (Including 51 Examples of Government Waste)," The Heritage Foundation, December 8, 2014, http://www.heritage.org/research/reports/2014/12/federal-spending-by-the-numbers-2014.

8   Ibid.

9   Elizabeth Rosenthal, "The Healthcare Waiting Game," The New York Times, July 5, 2014, http://www.nytimes.com/2014/07/06/sunday-review/long-waits-for-doctors-appointments-have-become-the-norm.html.

10   Berry, Mirabito, and Baun, "What's the Hard Return on Employee Wellness Programs?"

CHAPTER 3

CONTROLLING THE NUMBERS

Let's look at the numbers when it comes to the high cost of a reactive view of healthcare. You already know that chronic diseases—which, again, are controllable—are the main reason for increasing healthcare costs. People who have a chronic disease often cost their employers hundreds of thousands of dollars in claims. In fact, of every dollar that's spent on healthcare, $0.95 is on treatment and only $0.05 is on prevention.[1] What would the impact on claims be if more were spent on prevention?

According to the study titled, "The United States of Diabetes: Challenges and Opportunities in the Decade Ahead," 50 percent of Americans could have diabetes or be prediabetic by the year 2020. This equates to about $3.4 trillion in claims over the next decade. A recent study by UnitedHealth Group found that more than 50 percent of Americans could have diabetes or be prediabetic by the year 2020.[2] That equates to about $3.4 trillion in claims over the next decade, according to the study titled "The United States of Diabetes: Challenges and Opportunities in the Decade Ahead."[3]

Diabetes is one of the most preventable diseases. Most cases of adult-onset diabetes can be avoided by maintaining a healthy weight, exercising more, eating a healthy diet, and not smoking. Think about how that $3.4 trillion in claims affects employers when a large part of the population is not taking responsibility for preventing diabetes or keeping their diet in check.

We have the same issue with smokers. Smoking isn't considered a disease, but it certainly causes a lot of illnesses. According to the CDC, between 2000 and 2004, smoking costs the United States approximately $193 billion, including $96 billion in direct health-care expenditures and $97 billion in lost productivity.[4]

The Milken Institute conducted a groundbreaking study titled "An Unhealthy America: The Economic Burden of Chronic Disease— Charting a New Course to Save Lives and Increase Productivity and Economic Growth." The study found that seven chronic diseases impact the United States' economy to the tune of $1.3 trillion annually, of this amount, lost productivity totals $1.1 trillion per year in lost productivity.[5]

SEVEN CHRONIC DISEASES IMPACTING THE US ECONOMY

cancer, diabetes, hypertension, stroke, heart disease, pulmonary conditions and mental disorders

A 2014 update to the report found that the organization had underestimated the increase in costs in ensuing years by more than $28 billion.[6] This unexpected cost, the institute reported, would be due to the increasing prevalence of these preventable, chronic conditions among Americans.[7] These numbers are staggering, and they're the reason we're trying to educate people about how chronic diseases are affecting us as a society.

THE CAUSE OF THE BULK OF THE PROBLEMS IN THE UNITED STATES

Anthony Wisniewski, the Executive Director of Health Policy for the US Chamber of Commerce and founder and co-chair of the US Workplace Wellness Alliance, said, "The combination of the aging US workforce, chronic disease, and the market crisis led to a situation where healthcare costs must be addressed immediately to avoid increased taxes, reduced benefits, or draining other vital programs to pay for healthcare."[8]

Wisniewski validates exactly what we're saying: If we don't take charge today, the costs of healthcare will impact every aspect of our lives. Every service that we have will be affected.

Average consumers may not realize the effects healthcare costs have on everyday life. The shoes they buy, the food they purchase, and the repairs they have on their home or car are all going to cost more due to higher healthcare costs caused by an unhealthy population.

If we as a country do not regulate the elements of our health that are within our control (such as chronic diseases), it will be difficult to maintain our current position in the global market. For instance, we've seen the auto industry have to increase the cost of their cars by approximately $1,500 to cover costs associated with increases to their company health insurance.[9] Imagine if that were to happen to every industry or business, because healthcare costs have gotten so out of control.

The ACA came about, in part, as a result of Americans needing a way to control the rising cost of healthcare after decades of neglecting personal health and preventive wellness. We need to remember that and continue the transformation from sick care to well care. I know we can make the transition because we've proven it possible by implementing wellness programs that educate employees in the workplace. We've seen the numbers; we've seen the ability to take an unhealthy employee population and transform it to a culture of preventative wellness. We've seen employees taking control of their bodies and taking control of their health, and we've seen the immediate change in the perception of how benefits are viewed.

Next, let's take a more in-depth look at the major chronic conditions that affect American employees and can be avoided, by and large, through education, early detection and actively managing your numbers.

HIGH BLOOD PRESSURE

A screening that reveals high blood pressure can lead to activities to reduce it and/or medication for employees to control the condition, helping them avoid heart attacks, strokes, and other ill effects of the disease.

Preventative medication costs less than treatment for a stroke or heart attack. Medications for high blood pressure may cost $20 or $30 a month, whereas a hospitalization for a heart attack can cost anywhere from $100,000 to $250,000.[10] If a person is aware of his or her condition and takes his or her medication properly, the employer ends up spending considerably less on prevention rather than tens of thousands of dollars in claims.

STRESS

Reducing stress leads to healthier, happier, more productive employees. If stress is not properly managed, it can result in lack of sleep, weight gain, anxiety, depression, and more. Battling stress is a matter of bringing everything back into balance, which means eating and sleeping well and controlling diseases like high blood pressure and diabetes.

Conversely, if people are not managing their chronic diseases, their stress levels will elevate, creating even more problems. Identifying and treating stress can help prevent many health issues.

HIGH CHOLESTEROL

We talk about cholesterol frequently, but many people don't really understand what it is. Basically, cholesterol is a waxy fat-like substance that is found in the cells of the body. Cholesterol can't dissolve in the blood. It must be transported through your bloodstream by carriers called lipoproteins, which got their name because they're made of fat (lipid) and proteins.

LDL cholesterol is considered the "bad" cholesterol because it contributes to plaque, a thick, hard deposit that can clog arteries and make them less flexible. This condition is known as atherosclerosis. If a clot forms and blocks a narrowed artery, heart attack or stroke can result.

HDL cholesterol is considered "good" cholesterol because it helps remove LDL cholesterol from the arteries. Experts believe HDL acts as a scavenger, carrying LDL cholesterol away from the arteries and back to the liver, where it is broken down and passed from the body. [11]

The two types of lipoproteins that carry cholesterol to and from cells are low-density lipoprotein, or LDL, and high-density lipoprotein, or HDL. While our bodies need some cholesterol, the wrong kind of cholesterol can build up in the arteries and slow the flow of blood.

A screening that reveals high cholesterol levels can lead to activities and/or medication to reduce cholesterol. Here again, medication combined with a healthy lifestyle is significantly more cost-effective and rewarding than the cost of hospitalization and rehabilitation for a stroke.

OBESITY

The paper "Obesity and Severe Obesity Forecasts Through 2030," which appeared in the *American Journal of Preventive Medicine*, estimates the cost of obesity to be $147 billion today.[12] What will that number look like in the future if we don't take action now?

According to John Cawley and Chad Meyerhoefer in the report "The Medical Care Costs of Obesity: An Instrumental Variables Approach," obesity-related illnesses account for approximately 21 percent of annual medical spending in the United States.[13] The aforementioned *American Journal of Preventive Medicine* obesity forecast paper estimated that, with a few "modestly successful obesity prevention efforts," potential savings in medical expenditures over the next two decades could reach $549.5 billion.[14]

In order to create these savings, employees diagnosed as obese, develop weight-loss plans with their doctors, who will help determine the most effective way to lose the weight. Every pound that an obese person loses makes him or her less of a risk for high-cost health problems and, more importantly, puts that person on the path to better health.

DIABETES

The cost of becoming a diabetic can range from the comparative pennies of the cost of prescriptions to tens of thousands of dollars in costs of care for all the diseases and conditions resulting from unmanaged diabetes. People diagnosed with diabetes have healthcare costs 2.3 times higher than if they didn't have the disease.[14]

Diabetes is one of the fastest-growing chronic diseases among children, and it is often linked with obesity, which puts increased demands on the body and its regulation of blood sugar. About 90 percent of people with type 2 diabetes are overweight or obese.[16] People that move from being obese to a healthier weight experience about a 25 percent reduction in health claims costs and a 32 percent reduction in workers' compensation and disability costs.[17]

Diagnosing and properly treating diabetes is essential to keeping one's health in check and preventing serious and costly diabetes-related complications such as damage to the eyes, heart, blood vessels, nervous system, teeth, gums, feet, skin, or kidneys. Properly preventing and managing diabetes is an effective way to avoid unnecessary healthcare costs that can negatively affect our economy.

SMOKING

Smoking causes approximately $75 billion in healthcare costs today. People who smoke are absent from work about twice as often as people who don't smoke, leading to a cost of about $27 billion.[18]

Cessation programs help participants gain a better understanding of how smoking affects the body. Cessation programs that succeed in helping people quit smoking can reduce healthcare costs by 17 percent.[19]

Smoking causes cancer of the lungs and other parts of the body, such as oral cancer, colorectal cancer, and many others. Smoking contributes to high blood pressure because it makes the arteries stiffer and narrower, causing the heart to work harder and blood pressure to increase. Smoking also causes blood clots, which can cause strokes and heart attacks.

Secondhand smoke (also known as environmental tobacco smoke) contains more than seventy substances that are causally linked to cancer. Even brief exposure to secondhand smoke can contribute to heart attacks, as the exposure causes platelets to become stickier and to aggregate.[20] It is estimated that in the United States, almost one in four children (ages three to eleven) lives in a home with at least one smoker. Children who live with a smoker are likely to inhale secondhand smoke, which increases their risk of developing health problems like pneumonia, bronchitis, and other lung diseases, as well as increased asthma attacks and ear infections. The effects of second-hand smoke are particularly harmful for young children and children with asthma. According to the American Academy of Otolaryngology–Head and Neck Surgery:

Exposure to environmental tobacco smoke (ETS) decreases lung efficiency and impairs lung function in children of all ages. It increases both the frequency and severity of childhood asthma. Secondhand smoke can aggravate sinusitis, rhinitis, cystic fibrosis, and chronic respiratory problems such as cough and postnasal drip. It also increases the number of children's colds and sore throats. In children under two, ETS exposure increases the likelihood of bronchitis and pneumonia.[21]

Children exposed to smoking also perceive smoking to be acceptable because they have grown up seeing parents or family members smoking. Smoking and tobacco products are still creating problems for generations to come. The best way to address smoking as an employer is to offer and incentivize smoking cessation programs that will improve employee health and result in long-term healthcare savings.

BREAST CANCER

Detecting breast cancer identified at stage I instead of stage IV saves lives—along with hundreds of thousands of dollars in healthcare costs.[22] According to The American Cancer Society's guidelines for early detection based on age, women twenty years old or older should perform breast self-examinations regularly and report any breast changes to their health professional right away. Women in their twenties and thirties should have a clinical breast exam as part of their regular health exam preferably every three years. And women forty and over should have a clinical breast exam by a health professional every year, in addition to a yearly mammogram[23].

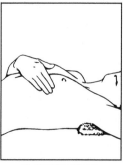
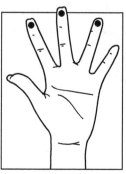
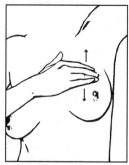

| Lie on your back with your arm behind your head. | Use the pads of your three middle fingers to feel the breast tissue using dime-sized, circular motions. | While standing, raise one arm. Using an up-and-down motion, examine from your sternum to your underarm, all the way down to your ribs. |

THE POWER OF EARLY BREAST CANCER DETECTION

I have worked in the Human Resources industry for over twenty-five years. Throughout my career, I've learned to apply a lot of what I share with my employees into my own life. Every time I sit with an employee to speak about their benefits, I remind them about the importance of their annual checkup. This message is something our employee benefits agency, Sapoznik Insurance, continuously stresses throughout the year, making a direct connection to prevention and medical claims reduction. Recently, I discovered first hand, exactly how fortunate I was to have followed my own advice.

During what I had thought to be just a regular, routine annual mammogram, something much more serious was discovered. My physician announced a devastating piece of news no one is ever prepared to hear: "You have breast cancer." The news was delivered, I'm certain, in a manner in which my physician had delivered countless times—as if simply stating the time of day. After allowing myself several moments to process what had just been revealed to me, my mind began to race. The questions arose and the concerns followed.

In the days following my diagnosis, the shock began to give way to gratitude that the cancer had been detected early through an exam that many women bypass due to lack of time or countless other reasons. In so many ways, the push for "early detection" Sapoznik Insurance and I so passionately promoted to my employees saved my life.

It is my own personal experience that an extremely busy work life makes keeping physician appointments difficult. I can tell you that, after my diagnosis, I will no longer play the "let's cross that bridge when I get to it" game.

Wellness is my new mantra, thanks to my current employer, Nature's Products, Inc., and Sapoznik Insurance, who partner to provide our on-site wellness biometrics and education, along with constant reminders of how important it is to remain aware of your health. Wellness is something we should all embrace. It is the food for life and preservation. Early detection saved my life, and I hope whoever reads this realizes that cancer or other medical issues do not discriminate.

Ampi Villar
Employee Benefits Administrator, Nature's Products

Breast cancer is a preventable disease that, according to the National Cancer Institute, one in eight women will be diagnosed within her lifetime. When it's detected early, the five-year survival rate is 98 percent, according to the National Breast Cancer Foundation.[24] Smart employers encourage and incentivize regular mammograms to help detect breast cancer early so that it can be treated quickly, saving time, money, and most importantly, lives.

ENVIRONMENT OF WELLNESS

In addition to testing for the aforementioned diseases and conditions, there are other tests that can keep us informed, such as prostate-specific antigen testing (for prostate cancer) and colonoscopies (for issues affecting the colon). There is a higher likelihood that employees will have these tests taken on their own if they work in an environment that promotes wellness.

In fact, when you create an environment of wellness within your organization, everyone becomes part of the solution. Coworkers tend to encourage and support each other to make changes that affect their health. They support fellow coworkers, whom they see nearly every day, and urge them to stop habits that are harmful to their health, such as smoking or eating unhealthy foods.

THE VALUE OF SCREENING

The simplest way for people to take responsibility for and control of their health is through biometric screening, which lets employees see what their numbers are and understand where those numbers should be. Those numbers are the target ranges for a variety of conditions in the human body, as established by the medical community. The numbers are based on a variety of factors, including age, sex, and height. For example, a screening usually starts with a person's weight: What is the employee's current weight (his or her number)? What should his or her weight be? Does that weight fall within the acceptable BMI range?

Making Sense of Your Biometric Numbers

Biometric screenings can provide a picture of your overall health. Your results indicate where you are today and help you set priorities for improving your health. Use this chart to learn what your biometric numbers mean. Discuss your results with your doctor or health-care provider if any of your values are outside of the normal range.

BIOMETRIC MEASURE	DESCRIPTION	VALUE RANGES*		GENERAL RECOMMENDATIONS
Total Cholesterol	Total cholesterol is the measurement of the different kinds of fat or lipids in your blood. Most fat comes from your diet.	<200 mg/dl	Desirable	Check your cholesterol and triglyceride levels every year.
		200 - 239 mg/dl	Borderline	
		240 mg/dl and above	High	
		My number:		
HDL Cholesterol	HDL is known as your "good" cholesterol because it carries cholesterol away from the arteries and out of your body, reducing your risk of heart disease.	<40 mg/dl	Low	
		40 - 59 mg/dl	Normal	
		60 mg/dl or higher	Optimal	
		My number:		
LDL Cholesterol	LDL is known as "bad" cholesterol because it clogs arteries and increases your risk of heart attack and stroke.	<100 mg/dl	Optimal	Healthy lifestyle habits like regular exercise and a diet high in whole grains, vegetables, and fruits and low in fat can help boost your HDL levels and lower your LDL and triglyceride levels.
		100 - 129 mg/dl	Near Optimal	
		130 - 159 mg/dl	Borderline High	
		160 - 189 mg/dl	High	
		190 mg/dl and above	Very High	
		My number:		
Triglycerides	A type of fat found in your blood. High triglyceride levels may contribute to hardening of the arteries, which increases your risk of stroke, heart attack, and heart disease.	<150 mg/dl	Normal	
		150 - 199 mg/dl	Borderline High	
		200 - 499 mg/dl	High	
		500 mg/dl and above	Very High	
		My number:		

BIOMETRIC MEASURE	DESCRIPTION	VALUE RANGES*		GENERAL RECOMMENDATIONS
Glucose	Glucose is your blood sugar. Blood glucose levels that remain high over time can damage the eyes, kidneys, nerves, and blood vessels. High glucose levels may also be an indicator of diabetes.	<200 mg/dl	Desirable	If age 45 or older, check glucose levels every three years if within normal ranges. If outside of normal ranges, check levels every year or more often as recommended by your doctor. Glucose testing for pre-diabetes and type 2 diabetes should be considered for any adult who is overweight and has more than one risk factor for diabetes.
		200 - 239 mg/dl	Borderline	
		240 mg/dl and above	High	
		My number:		
Blood Pressure	When your heart beats, it pumps blood through your arteries and creates pressure in them. The higher number (systolic) represents the pressure while your heart is beating. The lower number (diastolic) represents the pressure when your heart is resting between beats. Hypertension, or high blood pressure, increases your risk of developing heart disease and stroke.	<40 mg/dl	Low	Check your blood pressure every two years if you are below 120/80. If your systolic or diastolic is higher than normal, check your blood pressure every year. Dietary changes and exercise can lower your blood pressure. If you are living a healthy lifestyle and still have high blood pressure, your doctor may prescribe medicine
		40 - 59 mg/dl	Normal	
		60 mg/dl or higher	Optimal	
		My number:		
Body Mass Index (BMI)	BMI is an indicator of fat for most people. If you are very muscular, you may have a high BMI but not have a high percentage of body fat. BMI is calculated based on your height and weight. Being overweight or obese increases the risk of having high blood pressure, heart disease, stroke, diabetes, arthritis, breathing problems and certain types of cancer.	Adult BMI Categories:		If your weight is outside of normal ranges, increase physical activity and eat healthfully to shed pounds and control your weight.
		Underweight =<18.5		
		Normal Weight = 18.5-24.9		
		Overweight = 25-29.9		
		Obesity = BMI of 30 or greater		
		My number:		

*Triglycerides and glucose can increase greatly after eating. In order to ensure accuracy for the biometric screening, you are encouraged to fast (not eat or drink) for nine hours prior to screening. You may drink water.

Sources: American Heart Association; US Department of Health and Human Services; American Diabetes Association; National Heart Lung and Blood Institute

Weight is the first number that people need to understand, and they need to understand that their weight has a direct correlation to many of the chronic illnesses.[25] Also, it's pretty easy for people to monitor their weight with the purchase of a home scale.

The next number to understand is blood pressure. Like measuring your weight, it's very simple to measure your blood pressure. Today, people can walk into any pharmacy and use a machine to take their blood pressure for free.

When we implement our biometric screenings for employers for the first time, we normally find a number of people who have no idea that their blood pressures are so out of control that they are at high risk of experiencing a stroke or heart attack. As a matter of fact, many times we have to send people to the doctor for a checkup right away. Sometimes, we've even sent them straight to the emergency room, and as a result, they've avoided a heart attack or stroke because they were finally on the road to getting medications and bringing their hypertension under control.

Another number we measure is blood glucose. All it takes is a simple prick of the finger to let a person know if he or she is borderline diabetic. From a claims perspective, the difference between becoming a diabetic and not becoming a diabetic is tens of thousands of dollars. Again, a simple finger prick can let people know that they're at risk, and then a few easy changes in diet can help them avoid this detrimental, long-term illness.

If you look at the pie chart, in 2007, only 23 percent of all American workers had no chronic diseases. Another 22 percent had only one chronic disease, meaning that less than half (45 percent) had one or no chronic diseases. Meanwhile, nearly one-fifth (19 percent) had five or more chronic diseases.

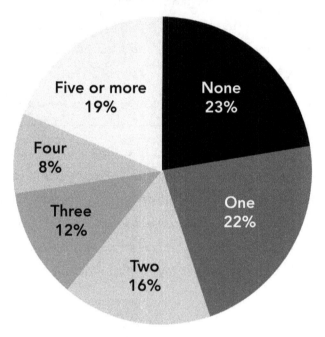

Chronic Disease Prevalence Among American Workers, 2007

Five or more 19%

None 23%

Four 8%

Three 12%

One 22%

Two 16%

Source: Newsweek Web Exclusive

The CDC estimates that by eliminating three risk factors—poor diet, inactivity, and smoking—80 percent of heart disease, stroke, and type 2 diabetes would go away.

Overweight rates have been climbing in the past decade. Right now, about nine million kids (roughly one in six) between the ages of six and nineteen are overweight. That number has quadrupled in the last thirty years. If we continue with these trends, one in three children who were born in the year 2000 will be overweight and develop diabetes.[26] In chapter 7, you'll find an exciting and innovative way that one school in Florida is combating this trend.

We are producing the unhealthiest population ever. That is the journey that we're on right now, and it's starting with our children. It's time to start a new journey and get employees and their families on the path to wellness—one of taking personal accountability for their health.

People really get caught up with their day-to-day lives, and often because of things that are beyond their control, it's hard for them to get in front of a doctor, which makes it hard for them to get preventive screenings.

That's why we bring the screenings to the workplace. We give employees their numbers and the information they need to get started on their journey of taking responsibility for their wellness. Once people find out that they have high blood pressure, are borderline diabetic, or are considered to be obese, we find that, many times, they take action.

At a cost of between $45 and $100 per employee, workplace screenings are among the wisest investments an employer may implement. That small investment can save significant dollars in claims and positively impact your bottom line.

SCREENING SAVES LIVES

We've seen employees significantly increase their participation in the biometric screening portion of our program when it's made readily available to them. For example, Nature's Products Inc., which manufactures and sells private-label supplements, vitamins, nutritional products, and the like, wanted their employees to be representative of its brand. The company wanted its team to be healthy.

We delivered a very robust health and wellness program on-site at that company's corporate office. The program included biometric screening for blood glucose levels, blood pressure, BMI, etc. and other activities such as acupuncture, chiropractic care (for spinal health), and massage therapy (to help with employees' day-to-day stress).

We also worked in partnership with a local hospital to bring in a mobile vehicle equipped with the latest mammography technology. This proved to be an invaluable service for one employee of the company, a woman in her early forties, when the mammogram detected stage I breast cancer.

Needless to say, she was alarmed, but she immediately went for treatment and experienced a successful outcome. Today, she credits the early-detection mammogram with saving her life. And she credits Sapoznik Insurance for the "foresight to make such an important screening available."

That's key to our programs: we bring them to the workplace and make them accessible on-site and during business hours, allowing employees to begin to get a grasp of their health situation in only a few minutes' time.

CASE STUDY: NATURE'S PRODUCTS

Nature's Products, established in 1986, is a world leader in the manufacturing of nutritional supplements. Working with Sapoznik Insurance, Nature's Products implemented a wellness program that resulted in a spirit of workplace camaraderie centered on health awareness and account-ability. The program was designed to be easy, was individualized to each employee, and included a timeline for ROI.

We started this journey three years ago. The CEOs of both Sapoznik Insurance and Nature's Products, Rachel Sapoznik and Jose Minski respectively, met to discuss the importance of healthy employees. When Nature's Products became a client of Sapoznik Insurance, they were just starting to think about improving their wellness initiatives. We were able to meet with the Nature's Products team— the CEO, human resources, and wellness consultant—to determine how they could begin to build the foundation for a wellness program. The goal was to address the needs of their employees, increase participation, and reduce claims.

Sapoznik's Wellness Team, together with their wellness consultant and with the participation of the employees of Nature's Products, was able to provide the resources to implement educational seminars, sponsor health fairs, and improve the quality of fitness classes offered. As an example, we implemented the Tobacco Cessation program, and now they have a smoke-free campus.

More than 70 percent of Nature's Products employees took part in the program. Activities the company implemented included signing a Wellness Commitment Letter as an agreement to participate in two or more wellness programs, educating them about simple tips for healthier living, and distributing information about losing weight, quitting smoking, and avoiding diabetes. Other events included the following:

- A mammogram van

- A "man van" that featured men's health services, including PSA testing

- A Use the Stairs program, which required employees to pay $1 for using the elevator without a good reason

- A health fair, featuring biometric screenings

- Seminars and on-site fitness programs

- Boot camps and walk/runs

- Massage therapy and healthy shakes

By educating and empowering the workplace community to make healthy choices, we are improving employee morale and performance, reducing employee absenteeism and preventing catastrophic health issues. Since the implementation of the wellness program, Nature's Products cumulatively, over a three-year period, reduced claims by 10 percent and substantially reduced heart disease related claims.

Nature's Products has received both local and national recognition for their commitment to the health and wellness of their employees. They care about wellness not only through their high-quality nutritional products but also with the wellness programs they provide to the employees in their organization. In 2015, the company was honored with three prestigious awards:

- **2015 Florida Worksite Wellness Award**

- **2015 Gold Level Recipient of the American Heart Association's Fit-Friendly Worksite Award**

- **2015 South Florida Business Journal's Healthiest Employer (Medium Company Category)**

There are many companies out there that have structured wellness programs; because every employer's dynamic is different, we look for the best programs for each employer. The key is to have a quarterback to work in harmony with your organization to create an environment of wellness. This only happens when the leadership team is committed to the program. By creating an environment in the workplace where wellness, healthy eating, and exercise are part of the culture, your employees will begin the paradigm shift.

FOCUS ON MENTAL HEALTH AND EMOTIONAL WELLNESS

Today's corporate wellness programs are mostly focused on helping employees improve their health by creating improvement initiatives around certain clinical measures. These measures include blood pressure, BMI, cholesterol, glucose, and smoking cessation.

Achieving and maintaining adequate levels can help prevent cancer, heart disease, diabetes, hypertension, and other illnesses that are known to drive up healthcare costs.

In addition, programs can include the oft-overlooked areas of mental health and emotional wellness. Although mental health is not as easily measured as blood pressure or cholesterol, organizations are finding that it deserves equal attention, especially when considering the costs associated with poor mental and emotional health. Absenteeism, loss of productivity, job abandonment, and higher rates of turnover are often directly linked to poor mental health.

Research suggests that people with symptoms of depression have a fivefold or greater increase in time lost from work compared to those without symptoms of depression, according to Jeffrey Kahn, MD, and Alan Langlieb, MD, in their book, *Mental Health and Productivity in the Workplace: A Handbook for Organizations and Clinicians.*[27]

A great way employers can begin to focus on employees' mental health is by ensuring that their benefits plans have access to mental health benefits, including an employee assistance program (EAP). EAPs are useful in that they can provide referrals to mental health professionals and other services while maintaining strict standards of confidentiality. Employers that offer mental health benefits are at a significant advantage over those who do not, as they are likely to have lower reported incidents of job burnout, workplace violence, and workplace injuries.

According to Virgin Pulse, "American business is reaching a tipping point where, left unmanaged, preventable health care costs are becoming one of the largest drains on their income statements.

Some studies show that at the current rate, 1/3 or more of many companies operating profits may be lost over the next 10 years based solely on the rising cost of healthcare, if they cannot reduce costs or increase prices for their goods and services. And, those costs don't just threaten company profitability. They threaten jobs, and the livelihoods of our employees.

The amount companies have to pay for health care coverage of their employees has been rising at nearly 10% per annum. And, over 75% of those costs are attributable to preventable chronic diseases, including: heart disease, diabetes and some forms of cancer.

Medical and productivity impact:

- Account for 75% ($1.5 trillion) of U.S. health care costs
- Lost economic output caused by 7 most prevalent chronic diseases totals more than $1 trillion
- Obese employees cost U.S. private employers $45+ billion annually in medical expenditures and work loss" [28]

U.S. employers and employees are paying for the high costs of chronic disease through the increase in health costs associated with greater demand for and use of health care services. Health care premiums for employer-sponsored family coverage have increased by 87 percent since 2000.

Health care coverage costs for people with a chronic condition average $6,032 annually, which is five times higher than for those without such a condition. [29]

A COMPETITIVE EDGE

Simply put, it's more expensive for everyone when workers are unhealthy and don't take responsibility for their health. According to *USA Today*, General Motors, Ford, and Chrysler spend more on employee health expenses than on the steel they use to make cars, and the cost of providing healthcare added between $1,000 and $1,500 to the cost of each of the 4.65 million vehicles General Motors sold in 2004.[30]

It's a chain reaction: the incremental cost of products, services, and every other aspect of our lives is affected by the higher costs of healthcare. Something has to give. Businesses have budgets, and they have cost-containment strategies. The cost of providing healthcare benefits to employees is central to cost analyses. Healthcare is front and center when it comes to deciding on the price for which you're going to sell your product or service.

That doesn't bode well from a competitive standpoint. Any product you're selling will likely be higher priced than your competitors' products if those companies have their healthcare costs under control and you don't. If you're not offering another reason to buy your product or service, higher pricing will negatively impact sales and your bottom line.

As the ACA becomes fully engaged in 2016, its mandate that employers with fifty or more employees must provide insurance (or be penalized) will have a real impact on businesses. Healthcare is a real cost, and there is no way around it. If you do not engage now in understanding the effects of wellness and the importance of shifting your employees' mind-set, you will be priced out of the market.

Employers that understand this, are engaged in making the change, and are implementing an environment of responsibility will have a competitive advantage in many areas. They're going to have a competitive advantage in terms of lower healthcare costs and better-performing, healthier, more productive employees. That, in turn, means a competitive advantage in production output and in streamlining the products they're selling or the services they're providing.

With healthcare now entwined in our daily business, forward-thinking, responsible CEOs and their respective leadership teams are the ones who will benefit the most from implementing wellness programs. By setting an example and helping their employees understand the necessity of a paradigm shift, CEOs can help lead the transition from treating illness to promoting wellness. Again, it is imperative that we move away from a reactionary approach to healthcare and into one that is progressive and preventive.

If you're a business owner who is appalled by your healthcare costs or concerned that, as of 2016, you're going to face healthcare expenses you've never encountered before—costs that are going to impact other areas of your organization—now is the time to act.

The penalties for noncompliance of the ACA are here. If you do nothing as an employer, penalties are going to be around $2,400 per employee. How are you passing on that cost? If you're planning to pass it on to the employee, then get ready for a wave of salary increase requests. That doesn't even account for the problems you're going to face when that employee and his family members have no insurance. How many people are going to leave for a company that does offer an affordable plan?

As an employer, if you're not actively planning how you will respond to these changes in healthcare policy, you're going to be in for a very difficult time.

1   Dean Ornish, "Yes, Prevention is Cheaper than Treatment," *Newsweek Web Exclusive*, April 24, 2008, accessed July 23, 2015, http://www.newsweek.com/health-prevention-worth-money-86075.

2   "The United States of Diabetes: Challenges and Opportunities in the Decade Ahead," UnitedHealth, November 2010, http://www.unitedhealthgroup.com/~/media/UHG/PDF/2010/UNH-Working-Paper-5.ashx.

3   Ibid.

4   "Smoking-Attributable Mortality, Years of Potential Life Lost, and Productivity Losses—United States, 2000–2004," Centers for Disease Control and Prevention, November 14, 2008, http://www.cdc.gov/mmwr/preview/mmwrhtml/mm5745a3.htm.

5   DeVol et al., "An Unhealthy America: The Economic Burden of Chronic Disease."

6   Chatterjee et al., "Checkup Time: Chronic Disease and Wellness in America."

7   Ibid.

8   "The Burden of Chronic Disease on Business and U.S. Competitiveness," Almanac of Chronic Disease 2009, https://www.prevent.org/data/files/News/pfcdalmanac_excerpt.pdf.

9   Julie Appleby and Sharon Silke Carty, "Ailing GM Looks to Scale Back Generous Health Benefits," *USA Today*, June 23, 2005, http://usatoday30.usatoday.com/money/autos/2005-06-22-gm-healthcare-usat_x.htm.

10   Cost Helper Health, "Heart Attack Treatment Cost," accessed September 28, 2015, http://health.costhelper.com/heart-attack-treatment-cost.html.

11   The American Heart Association, "Good vs. Bad Cholesterol," last modified April 21, 2014, http://www.heart.org/HEARTORG/Conditions/Cholesterol/AboutCholesterol/Good-vs-Bad-Cholesterol_UCM_305561_Article.jsp.

12   Eric A. Finkelstein et al., "Obesity and Severe Obesity Forecasts Through 2030," *American Journal of Preventive Medicine* 42 (June 2012) 6: 563-570, doi: http://dx.doi.org/10.1016/j.amepre.2011.10.026.

13   Cornell University. "Obesity accounts for 21 percent of U.S. healthcare costs, study finds." ScienceDaily. www.sciencedaily.com/releases/2012/04/120409103247.htm.

14   Finkelstein et al., "Obesity and Severe Obesity Forecasts Through 2030."

15   The Cost of Diabetes," American Diabetes Association, June 22, 2015, http://www.diabetes.org/advocacy/news-events/cost-of-diabetes.html?referrer=https://www.google.com/.

16   http://www.obesity.org/resources-for/your-weight-and-diabetes.htm

17   Laura Vanderkam, "Do Corporate Wellness Programs Really Boost Productivity?" Fast Company, accessed July 23, 2015, http://www.fastcompany.com/3033411/do-corporate-wellness-programs-really-boost-productivity.

18   William McDay and Heath Dingwell, *The Truth About Smoking*, (New York: DWJ Books LLC, 2009).

19   Fitch, Kate, Kosuke Iwasaki, Bruce Pyenson. "Covering Smoking Cessation as a Health Benefit: A Case for Employers," American Legacy Foundation, December 2006, accessed July 23, 2015, http://www.legacyforhealth.org/content/download/560/6767/file/Covering_Smoking_Cessation_as_a_Health_Benefit_-_A_Case_for_Employers.pdf.

20 Stanton Glantz and William Parmley, "Even a Little Secondhand Smoke is Dangerous," *JAMA* 286 (2001) 4: 462–463, doi:10.1001/jama.286.4.462, http://jama.jamanetwork.com/article.aspx?articleid=194033.

21 "Secondhand Smoke and Children," American Academy of Otolaryngology–Head and Neck Surgery, accessed July 23, 2015, https://www.entnet.org/content/secondhand-smoke-and-children.

22 "About Breast Cancer," National Breast Cancer Foundation, accessed July 23, 2015, http://www.nationalbreastcancer.org/breast-cancer-stage-0-and-stage-1.

23 "American Cancer Society recommendations for early breast cancer detection in women without breast symptoms," The American Cancer Society, accessed September 18, 2015, http://www.cancer.org/cancer/breastcancer/moreinformation/breastcancerearlydetection/breast-cancer-early-detection-acs-recs

24 National Breast Cancer Foundation, Inc., http://www.nationalbreastcancer.org/about-breast-cancer.

25 "Fast Facts: Obesity-Related Chronic Diseases," Stop Obesity Alliance, accessed July 26, 2015, http://www.stopobesityalliance.org/wp-content/themes/stopobesityalliance/pdfs/Fast%20Facts%20Chronic%20Disease%201-2012.pdf.

26 "Childhood Obesity Facts," Centers for Disease Control and Pervention," accessed September 28, 2015, http://www.cdc.gov/healthyschools/obesity/facts.htm.

27 Jeffrey Kahn and Alan Langlieb, *Mental Health and Productivity in the Workplace: A Handbook for Organizations and Clinicians* (San Francisco: Jossey-Bass, 2003).

28 http://www.virginpulse.com/blog-post/what-is-the-impact-of-chronic-disease-on-business/

29 http://www.justmeans.com/blogs/the-debilitating-costs-of-chronic-diseases-to-americas-future#sthash.l02nVZKc.dpuf

30 Appleby and Silke Carty, "Ailing GM Looks to Scale Back Generous Health Benefits."

CHAPTER 4

THE IMPACT OF DIET AND EXERCISE

Diet and exercise are crucial components to good health. Unfortunately, according to the President's Council on Fitness, Sports, & Nutrition, we're falling behind as a nation. Consider these statistics:

- Only one in three children is physically active every day.
- Fewer than 5 percent of adults participate in thirty minutes of physical activity every day.
- Only one in three adults receives the recommended amount of physical activity each week.
- 28 percent of Americans age six and older (80.2 million people) are physically inactive.
- A typical American's diet exceeds the recommended intake levels or limits in four categories: calories from solid fats and added sugars, refined grains, sodium, and saturated fat.

- Americans eat less than the recommended amounts of vegetables, fruits, whole grains, dairy products, and oils.
- Since the 1970s, the number of fast-food restaurants in the United States has more than doubled.
- Empty calories from added sugars and solid fats contribute to 40 percent of total daily calories for children between two and eighteen years old, and half of these empty calories come from six sources: soda, fruit drinks, dairy desserts, grain desserts, pizza, and whole milk.
- The United States' per capita total annual consumption of fat increased from approximately 57 pounds in 1980 to 78 pounds in 2009, with the highest consumption being 85 pounds in 2005.[1]

Initially, when we are working on a wellness program, we start with the numbers that help us evaluate the current state of the organization. This evaluation allows us to provide a blueprint for the wellness program. We follow up with reminders to encourage consistency, and then we suggest incentives to stimulate participation. Every program evolves over time as employees participate and begin to see change and as employers begin to see the effect on their bottom line.

For some, the idea of implementing a wellness program just seems too large and overwhelming a task. However, because we introduce changes incrementally, the wellness programs we design roll out in a natural progression that is neither burdensome nor overwhelming.

In other words, we don't suggest forcing an immediate about-face. We're not going to make employees who are extremely unhealthy change overnight. What we're looking to do is to get the human body to a better state of balance—to get people thinking about how to take responsibility for wellness. If a person sits all day long or doesn't move his or her body, it's not going to continue to function as well. Because fitness is crucial to overall health, we bring activities such as Zumba or yoga classes to the jobsite, or we present ideas that encourage people to team up and walk during lunch. The goal is to simply get people up and moving.

Imagine a vehicle: If the tires on the vehicle are not inflated, how efficiently will that vehicle operate? How much more gas will it use if it hasn't had regular maintenance? Similarly, the human body needs to operate like a well-oiled machine so that it can consistently perform at its optimum level.

But as employers, we have to allow employees time to work on healthier habits, and we have to instill in them a sense of responsibility. Once again, we as employers are going to benefit greatly from empowering our employees to develop healthy practices.

THE BURDEN OF WEIGHT

According to the CDC, "the estimated annual medical cost of obesity in the US was $147 billion in 2008 US dollars; the medical costs for people who are obese were $1,429 higher than those of normal weight."[2] Because of frequent health problems, obese individuals incur about 36 percent more in health services expenses and use about 77 percent more medications than average-sized people.[3] These additional costs affect not only those overweight and obese individuals but also the organizations that employ them.

Too often, people who are overweight think their poor health only affects themselves, but obesity is a universal concern because of the impact it continues to have on the US healthcare system. Employers are beginning to see the benefits of educating their employees about the dangers of obesity and are starting to implement programs that help their employees reach and maintain a healthy weight.

Nutritional intake makes all the difference. We have to move away from the idea of *diet* as a "four-letter word." The whole idea of *diet* already implies failure, because typically a diet is a temporary state. Taking responsibility is really about changing the way we think and changing the idea of immediate gratification. It's time to change the concept that people only go on a diet to lose weight; it's time to move to take responsibility for better food choices in order to have a healthier lifestyle.

That's why we work to educate people on how to view nutrition as a choice that is made every day, a choice that influences and forms behavior. Changing behavior works. Changing the way we view food works. Making better nutritional choices every day as part of a healthier lifestyle works. The healthy eating choices that become part of our lifestyle lead to healthier outcomes.

Insurance companies used to pay for gastric bypass surgery. This procedure was for very obese people and basically involved dividing an obese person's stomach in half so that he or she would eat less. But over the years, the failure rate of the procedure became astronomical: the obese people eventually put a considerable amount of weight back on. This was happening to the point that many insurance companies stopped covering the procedure because they weren't getting the success they anticipated. This happened, in part, because there was a lack of education about nutrition and behavioral change following the surgery. We want healthier, nutritional food choices to sustain the way people live their lives, as opposed to a diet that makes a temporary impact. People who have a more sustainable weight live longer and healthier lives.

CRAVING THIS	TRY THIS....

Sweet Breakfast Pastries

Looking for sweet? Try dessert flavored granola bars with way better ingredients and nutrients.

Ice Cream

Looking for creamy? Grab a protein packed Greek yogurt!

Potato Chips

Looking for salty? Try a serving of mixed nuts, air-popped popcorn, turkey jerky, crackers, and hummus!

Sodas

Looking for refreshing? Try coconut water! It's full of natural electrolytes with no sugar added.

Mac & Cheese

Looking for cheesy? Reach for part skim cheese and whole wheat crackers!

It's important to note that future generations are seeing and learning the behaviors of today's adults. Parents and guardians who are not exercising and are not making good, nutritional food choices are teaching children to make the same poor lifestyle choices. That's why we're seeing the increase of diabetes in children at the most astronomical rate that has even been seen in the history of the world.

According to an article published in *JAMA* (The Journal of American Medicine), obesity was the second-most-preventable cause of death in America in 2000, with smoking and alcohol ranking at first and third respectively.[4]

WHY ARE OTHER COUNTRIES HEALTHIER?

Other countries around the world tend to be healthier than the United States. Why? Diet and exercise. According to a Commonwealth Fund report, "Despite having the most expensive healthcare system, the United States ranks last overall among eleven industrialized countries on measures of health system quality, efficiency, access to care, equity, and healthy lives."[5]

In Europe, South America, and the Middle East, people eat more fresh fruits and vegetables than processed ones. They also eat more fish. There's no supersizing of fast-food orders. They're not drinking soda; they're drinking water. It's a completely different mind-set. There isn't the mind-set that they have to have fast food, because they only have five minutes to eat.

Some countries have gone so far as to tax unhealthy foods:

- Denmark introduced a tax on foods containing more than 2.3 percent saturated fats (meat, cheese, butter, edible oils, margarine, spreads, snacks, etc.) in 2011. Denmark had also increased its excise taxes on chocolate, ice cream, sugary drinks, and confectionery by 25 percent in 2010.

- In 2011, Hungary introduced a tax on selected manufactured foods with high sugar, salt, or caffeine content. Carbonated, sugary drinks are among the products targeted by the new measures. The tax does not concern basic foodstuffs and only affects products that have healthier alternatives.
- In France, a tax on soft drinks came into force in January 2012.[6]

Nutrition in other countries is a key component of their lifestyle. When they're eating breakfast, lunch, or dinner, they are present; they're enjoying the moment. Meals are a crucial part of their lifestyle. Unfortunately, many Americans are always on the run; they don't take the time to enjoy a meal. Our meals have to be big, fast, hot, and to-go.

In addition to eating better, people in other countries also tend to get more exercise. They walk and bike more, which is just the nature of living in centuries-old cities where it's easier to navigate tight, crowded streets on foot or by bicycle.

HEALTHY FOOD CHOICES MAKE A DIFFERENCE

As part of our program, we propose making better food choices a part of your corporate wellness strategy and suggest that you find ways to offer healthy alternatives during the workday.

For example, we encourage workers to stay away from sugars to avoid the eventual crash that comes with it. During the workday, many people add large amounts of sugar to their coffee or drink high-sugar drinks, which leads to headaches, upset stomach, grogginess, fatigue, and mood swings. So we really recommend avoiding sugar as much as possible to help improve productivity.

We suggest replacements such as nuts or fruit in place of foods containing processed sugar. And we live what we teach: at Sapoznik Insurance, we essentially forbid visitors or vendors from bringing in high-fat sweets such as donuts. We opt instead for natural snacks or snacks that are more in line with a healthy outcome. We've found that people just really seem to prefer healthier snacks.

Taking away an unhealthy choice (such as donuts) not only removes unnecessary fat and calories, it also removes the guilt factor that comes after. Bananas, apples, nuts, and other, healthier snacks make people feel more energized. We promote better choices by giving those better choices an opportunity to really prove to people that they are going to feel better once those better choices are made.

Part of our program includes working with employers and their employees to understand food labels. We work to educate people on how to read labels to understand sugar, sodium, fat, and other content levels. We want people to really understand what they are eating, and the only way they can do that is by understanding the labels on the food they are buying. We work to help people understand what they are reading when they are trying to make healthy decisions.

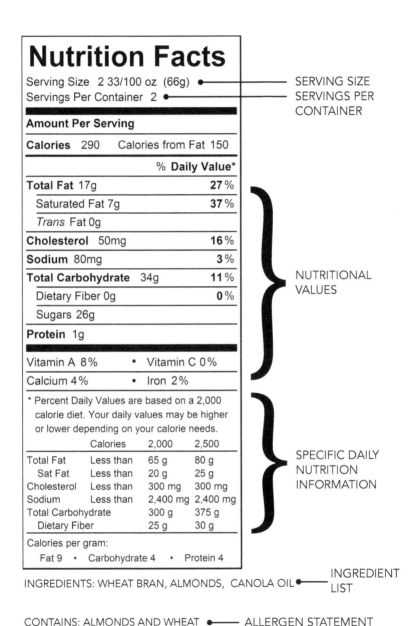

Nutrition Facts

Serving Size 2 33/100 oz (66g) ●————————— SERVING SIZE
Servings Per Container 2 ●————————— SERVINGS PER CONTAINER

Amount Per Serving

Calories 290   Calories from Fat 150

% **Daily Value***

Total Fat 17g	**27**%
Saturated Fat 7g	**37**%
Trans Fat 0g	
Cholesterol 50mg	**16**%
Sodium 80mg	**3**%
Total Carbohydrate 34g	**11**%
Dietary Fiber 0g	**0**%
Sugars 26g	
Protein 1g	

Vitamin A 8%   •   Vitamin C 0%

Calcium 4%   •   Iron 2%

NUTRITIONAL VALUES

* Percent Daily Values are based on a 2,000 calorie diet. Your daily values may be higher or lower depending on your calorie needs.

	Calories	2,000	2,500
Total Fat	Less than	65 g	80 g
Sat Fat	Less than	20 g	25 g
Cholesterol	Less than	300 mg	300 mg
Sodium	Less than	2,400 mg	2,400 mg
Total Carbohydrate		300 g	375 g
Dietary Fiber		25 g	30 g

Calories per gram:
  Fat 9   •   Carbohydrate 4   •   Protein 4

SPECIFIC DAILY NUTRITION INFORMATION

INGREDIENTS: WHEAT BRAN, ALMONDS, CANOLA OIL ●——— INGREDIENT LIST

CONTAINS: ALMONDS AND WHEAT ●——— ALLERGEN STATEMENT

EXERCISE IN THE WORKPLACE

"Sitting disease," as it's come to be known, is growing at a rapid rate. Women are at the most risk because they are more likely to lead a sedentary life.[7]

The average American spends eleven hours every day sitting. Think about that: eleven hours. That is a scary statistic. In large part it's because 80 percent of the American workforce does little or no physical activity at work; they are at their desks, where they are not engaged in any physical activity.[8] And those sedentary lifestyles result in US healthcare expenditures of $24 billion annually.[9]

What's even scarier is that a 2004 study, conducted by the University of Hong Kong and the Department of Health, found that 20 percent of all deaths of people age thirty-five and older could be attributed to a lack of physical activity and exercise.[10]

People become very sedentary when they are at work. Since we live in an age of technology, people don't have to get up from their desks to get files anymore; documents are on the network or are e-mailed, and they can be retrieved via a computer, a smartphone, or a tablet. There is no more real movement inside an office these days.

TIPS FOR MOVING WHILE AT WORK

- Stand whenever possible, such as when talking on the phone.

- Park farther away from the door.

- Take stretching breaks.

- Participate in on-site fitness demos or classes.

- Play in corporate sports leagues.

- Ask for a standing or walking desk.

- Work out over your lunch break.

- Compete in challenges using wearable devices such as pedometers.

- Charge elevator taxes. To encourage employees to use the stairs, some companies are placing a box or jar to collect an "elevator tax" from anyone using the elevator. The funds later go toward wellness initiatives, healthy snacks, or charitable contributions.

- Hold walking meetings. Instead of sitting around a boardroom, some companies are having meetings and huddles in groups while walking around designated areas of the building or office campus.

Inactivity costs between $670 and $1,125 per person per year.[11] This is an entirely preventable figure. Along with a proper diet, regular exercise can dramatically reduce the occurrence of heart disease, stroke, and other health issues. Unfortunately, according to the CDC, nearly 80 percent of American adults don't get the government-recommended amount of weekly exercise. The CDC recommends 2.5 hours of moderate-intensity aerobic activity or 1 hour and 15 minutes of vigorous-intensity activity per week.[12]

While it's not really up to the company leaders or managers to keep employees fit, it is up to them to get the best results in order to maximize employee productivity and efficiency. Considering how key fitness is to overall health, it's worth implementing fitness programs in the workplace, where so many of us spend a significant portion of our lives. We often implement walking clubs as part of the wellness programs we bring to the workplace, which is just one of the many ways an organization can encourage movement in the workplace.

Another way to encourage more movement is to start monitoring activities around the clock with activity trackers. Wearable technology monitors come in a variety of models and include features such as the ability to track steps, calories, walking or running distance, heart rate, and sleep.

We've found that there is an increase in movement when employers and their employees are using these wearable devices on the job. The devices promote movement and serve as reminders to walk a little more than you otherwise would; they're an easy, inexpensive way to get in the habit of moving and not remaining sedentary.

What we've found through our programs (and according to a study presented by the American College of Sports Medicine) is that workers who get thirty to sixty minutes of exercise during lunch have a higher performance level during the rest of the day.[13] The study found that workers' performance levels were boosted by as much as 15 percent.[14] It didn't matter what type of exercise they did—either walking, running, yoga, or another activity.

Movement within an office (such as taking the stairs instead of the elevator) increases a person's productivity. Moving around can take away that post-lunch low that many people experience and can also improve the overall mood around the office.

There are also longer-term benefits of allowing employees to be active, including reduced absenteeism and more vitality in the workplace. Healthy, active employees take fewer sick days and bring more energy to work. According to a 2011 study published in the *Journal of Occupational and Environmental Medicine*, allowing employees to engage in just 2.5 hours of exercise per week during the work day produced a noticeable reduction in absenteeism.[15]

Some employers resist the idea of an employee taking a few minutes longer to accomplish a task—for example, taking the stairs instead of the elevator or walking to someone's desk rather than sending an email—until they understand that they are the greatest beneficiaries. In addition to greater employee satisfaction at work, employers tend to be the most satisfied because there is greater productivity, better outcomes, better work quality, and a drop in absenteeism.

All of these things greatly contribute to a better work environment, which means healthier employees and greater profits. Brain functions go up, and everything improves exponentially when employees incorporate more movement in their day.

TIME TO TAKE RESPONSIBILITY

It's time for people to take personal responsibility for their health and wellness. Whenever we are implementing any of these programs, whether we're promoting healthy eating and exercise or wellness in the workplace, it's imperative to have employer participation. Studies have shown over and over again that taking part in trackable activities—from walking groups to weight-loss contests—increases employees' productivity. And by increasing employee productivity, the employer is going to see not only higher profits but also a healthier workforce, which is going to reduce the company's overall health costs.

Exercise is a clear win for companies in terms of health, morale, and productivity. Considering how much time people spend in the office and how pervasive chronic and preventable diseases are, it's time to recognize that the future of individuals, companies, and communities may well depend on how much physical activity people do in the workplace.

It's time for employers to change their assumption that employees who aren't glued to their desks aren't being productive; instead, with physical activity in the workplace, when those employees *are* at their desks, they're more productive because they're healthier, happier, and more alert.

At the end of the day, people want to work where they feel they're making a difference. By allowing them to take part in a little more activity, they will produce better work, make fewer mistakes, provide better customer service, and have better attitudes. Satisfaction goes up, and turnover goes down. They are going to be much better employees, and your organization will benefit from it.

Companies that have embraced the concept of a well-balanced work environment that includes healthy eating and exercise are some of the world's fastest-growing companies. Just look at Google and Zappos: these companies have allotted time for employees to exercise, meditate and have integrated wellness activities into their organization.

1   "Facts & Statistics," President's Council on Fitness, Sports & Nutrition, accessed July 23, 2015, http://www.fitness.gov/resource-center/facts-and-statistics/#footnote-1.

2   "Adult Obesity Facts," Centers for Disease Control and Prevention," accessed July 23, 2015, http://www.cdc.gov/obesity/data/adult.html.

3   "Obesity and Disability: The Shape of Things to Come," Rand Corporation, accessed July 23, 2015, http://www.rand.org/pubs/research_briefs/RB9043-1/index1.html.

4   Ali Mokdad et al., "Actual Causes of Death in the United States, 2000," *JAMA* 291 (2004) 10: 1238–45, doi:10.1001/jama.291.10.1238, http://jama.jamanetwork.com/article.aspx?articleid=198357.

5   Mary Mahon and Bethanne Fox, "US Health System Ranks Last Among Eleven Countries on Measures of Access, Equity, Quality, Efficiency, and Healthy Lives," The Commonwealth Fund, June 16, 2014, http://www.commonwealthfund.org/publications/press-releases/2014/jun/us-health-system-ranks-last.

6   "Obesity Update 2012," OECD, accessed July 23, 2015, http://www.oecd.org/health/49716427.pdf.

7   David Sturt and Todd Nordstrom, "Is Sitting the New Smoking?" *Forbes*, January 13, 2015, http://www.forbes.com/sites/davidsturt/2015/01/13/is-sitting-the-new-smoking/.

8   Mandell, Lisa Johnson. "America Becomes Desk Potato Nation," Aol Jobs, May 27, 2011, accessed July 23, 2015, http://jobs.aol.com/articles/2011/05/27/america-becomes-desk-potato-nation/.

9   Michael Pratt, Caroline A. Macera, and Guijing Wang, "Higher Direct Medical Costs Associated With Physical Inactivity," *The Physician and Sportsmedicine* 28, no. 10 (Oct 2000).

10 Mike Adams, "Sedentary Lifestyle Causes More Deaths than Smoking, Says Study," Natural News, July 28, 2004, http://www.naturalnews.com/001547.html#ixzz3UmSnLUVh.

11 "The Financial Impact of Improved Health Behaviors," Rutgers New Jersey Agricultural Experiment Station, accessed July 23, 2015, https://njaes.rutgers.edu/healthfinance/health-behaviors.asp.

12 "How Much Physical Activity Do Adults Need?" Centers for Disease Control and Prevention, accessed July 23, 2015, http://www.cdc.gov/physicalactivity/everyone/guidelines/adults.html.

13 Jacqueline Stenson, "Exercise May Make You a Better Worker," NBCNews.com, July 12, 2005, http://www.nbcnews.com/id/8160459/ns/health-fitness/t/exercise-may-make-you-better-worker/.

14 Ibid.

15 Ryan Holmes, "Why Companies Should Get Serious about Working Out at Work," *Financial Post*, October 7, 2014, http://business.financialpost.com/2014/10/07/why-companies-should-get-serious-about-working-out-at-work/?__lsa=c463-c70c.

CHAPTER 5

THE WELLNESS PROGRAM BLUEPRINT

E very day, employees face the risk of developing chronic diseases. No employee is immune to these risks. The risk of heart disease, high blood pressure, osteoporosis, diabetes, obesity, and some cancers can be reduced by incorporating healthy behaviors such as physical activity, good nutrition, and stress reduction into our daily lives. You and your leadership team have the power to take control of escalating healthcare costs by changing how employees manage these health risks and ensuring personal accountability. Employers are recognizing that it is good business to help their employees make healthier lifestyle choices. By providing a supportive environment that offers access to health education programs, value-based benefits, safe and health-friendly facilities, and sound policies, employers can improve the health and productivity of their employees which will have positive effects on the organization's bottom line. They also create a healthier business in more than one sense of the phrase.

This chapter describes our 3-Year Employee Wellness Plan and provides an outline that can be used to comprehensively assess, plan, and implement programs, policies, and changes in almost any work environment.

WHY WORKSITE WELLNESS?

Developing an employee wellness plan will reduce costs and absenteeism. It will improve employee engagement and make the workforce an active part of the solution to rising healthcare expenses. Offering employees a chance to improve their quality of life presents a unique chance for employers to positively impact the people who spend their days doing the work of the organization.

Let's begin by taking a closer look at our strategic approach to planning a wellness program, which starts with a Personal Health Assessment (PHA), gathering a baseline measurement for each employee.

THE 3-YEAR WELLNESS TIMELINE AND STRATEGY

The Sapoznik 3-Year Worksite Wellness Plan is designed to effectively and collaboratively address priorities to improve employees' overall health in order to reduce health costs and ultimately shift the company culture from reactive to proactive. Science-based strategies are used to reach employees and their families. The healthy culture that emerges over three years will demonstrate that the organization and its employees have shifted into a culture of proactive wellness and health.

The top key areas of focus for reducing healthcare costs are described below.

GOAL	OBJECTIVE
Support corporate culture that encourages healthy lifestyles.	• Identify a wellness champion and appoint a wellness manager with defined wellness responsibilities. • Form a Wellness Team with clearly defined membership, budget, and goals. • Conduct a health needs assessment. • Execute and evaluate an ongoing wellness plan.
Reduce medical cost trends using claims data, and identify the most costly medical condition for population-based support or intervention.	• Evaluate change in condition management as a result of the wellness program.
Maximize participation in PHA and wellness programs.	• Implement an annual PHA with incentive to achieve a minimum of a 75% participation rate. • Integrate PHA into new-hire orientation by (date). • Offer PHA as a prerequisite to employee benefits by (date).
Increase productivity through reduced absenteeism, improved presenteeism.	• Achieve a 10% reduction in sick leave over two years.
Encourage employees to be more physically active.	• Organize walking club and provide incentives by (date). • Implement stair use program by (date). • Design flexible work policy so employees can participate in physical fitness activities without interfering with business needs by (date). • Secure discounted fitness center memberships by (date).

YEAR ONE: THE FIRST STEPS

The first key steps of the wellness program are research and planning. This represents one of the most important areas to your program's success as it creates an opportunity to assess and uncover the needs of your employees. It is at this critical phase that we also seek senior management buy in as it is part of the strategy to promote and support the implementation of wellness at an organization. Leadership buy in and engagement is crucial to successful outcomes.

The tasks we must first focus on involve fact-finding and assessing needs, which include:

- Coordinating with the leadership team and employees for input on health interests and needs
- Reviewing outcomes from previous wellness initiative (if any)
- Setting goals
- Developing a budget for wellness activities and incentives

After gathering the information, it is time to determine and schedule the events and activities that will be implemented for the year. Keeping in mind that variation, and diversity in programming will help stimulate interest in your employees and capture the attention of a wide range of people. Some are challenged by the thrill of competition, others want to accomplish goals as a team. Your team member needs are diverse, your wellness program should aim to address those diverse needs.

Our plan suggests establishing a formal announcement of your wellness program with the creation of a letter signed by the CEO that articulates his or her belief that health and wellness are crucial elements of the work environment. This is also the perfect moment to enhance communication through strategically placed flyers, banners, posters and emails that will help spread the message of wellness. This is a wonderful way to let employees feel how much their employer cares about their health.

Once this communication campaign is underway, we begin to execute programming based on discoveries during the research and planning phase.

When we put together a program, we work in conjunction with the company's leadership team to create ongoing educational pieces that encourage employees to move in a healthy direction. The Wellness Program Planning Template shown on the next page is a resource recommended by the Mayo Clinic, that we often use with our clients when outlining their customized plan. The template allows us to define the purpose and goals of the program, which will determine the program's content and how we will evaluate its effectiveness.

During the first year, we also form a wellness team led by influential employees who work within the strategy that we put together to motivate and stimulate a competitive, yet fun, environment. Just like any other program you implement for your business, it's important to create very specific goals and programs to reach those goals.

WELLNESS PROGRAM PLANNING TEMPLATE

Section 1: General Information

Program Overview

A brief overview of the organization's program should describe its overall purpose and goal. This is a critical area addressed in year one: stating what the organization is attempting to accomplish by implementing the program.

Example: The (name of organization) employee wellness program is a voluntary program of structured activities for its team members, designed to stabilize the company's healthcare costs. Through this wellness program, you become a part of the solution in controlling these costs, improving the group's general level of health and positively impacting the bottom line.

Participation Requirements

The organization's policies and procedures, such as personnel policies, should be considered and explicitly stated in the program plan.

Example: Eligibility requirements

1. Describe the eligibility for voluntary or mandatory participation for employees (full-time and part-time) in program activities.

2. Describe the eligibility of spouses and other immediate family members.

Employee Assessment

Evidence that employees' needs and interests have been considered in planning program objectives should be included to help determine what programs to offer. Employees' needs and interests should be assessed to assist planners in identifying what, when, and how employees will access wellness programs. Other assessments can provide insight into people's lifestyle habits and health claims, providing the ability to target programs at the employees with the most pressing needs. A description of the information learned in these assessments will provide justification to management for the implementation of specific activities.

Examples: survey tools, focus groups, health risk assessments, health claims data review

Use of Facilities

A description of the use of available facilities for health, fitness, or educational programs should be included to provide guidance on what is allowable at the worksite.

Providers of Instruction/Services

An organization may consider contracting with qualified providers of instruction and services related to their program. Qualified personnel within an organization may also be available to serve as health fitness instructors and activity leaders, when appropriate. If internal employees are allowed to provide services, the organization should state any limitations regarding the use of work time to provide those services.

Examples: local, state, or federal agencies, hospitals, medical care professionals, health educators, nutritionists, dietitians, exercise physiologists, community organizations, consultants, other individuals or groups with expertise in health fitness

Section 2: Program Content

Your company's wellness program content can be as unique as your organization. That uniqueness results in a terrific opportunity for customization of your strategies. Always take into account factors that can affect employee engagement such as: time for conducting wellness activities, for example, before, during or after work hours.

Informal program activities might consist of intramural sports or various types of employee club activities that may include walking, jogging or group exercise classes. Generally, informal activities are coordinated by employees with a special interest in some aspect of a health-related topic. Some activities can also include organized sports such as softball, tennis or kickball. Since these activities are elective in nature and by no means mandatory, they are not necessarily included as part of an organization's formal employee wellness program. Participation in these types of activities should be incentivized and recognized by the employer whenever possible.

When developing the program content, review the employee assessment information gathered from your focus groups or surveys to determine which activities will produce the desired effect for your program.

Program Objectives, Expected Results, and Evaluation

The primary goal of each organization's program should be stated clearly so that both management and employees understand the reason for investing their time and resources in the activities. The objective should revolve around controlling the costs of healthcare for the entire organization. It is important to reiterate that support from the leadership team is essential. This is a key part of a successful wellness strategy because of the time it takes to gather quantifiable data while taking into account variables such as turnover, new hires, and behavioral modification.

The organization's plan should include measurable objectives, which allow you to identify positive traction, or conversely, areas that still need improvement. Objectives in three categories (process, impact, and outcome) should be included:

- **Process objectives** are measurable, short-term statements of what the program will do, such as: "By month/year, the employee wellness program will recruit 50 percent of the employees to participate in a health screening/health fair to increase their knowledge about health risks and healthy behaviors."

- **Impact objectives** are measurable, mid-term statements of what the program expects to happen as a result of its activities, such as: "By month/year increase the number of annual physical exams and preventive medical visits with primary physicians for the company by 25%."

- **Outcome objectives** are measurable, long-term statements of what the program expects will result from the implementation of the program, such as: "Positively bend the medical claims cost curve for the organization and remain 10% below national medical trend costs."

Evaluation

The program plan should address program evaluation. Plans for evaluating the program will be made when the program objectives are set.

Metrics should be selected to allow the organization to determine if its objectives were met. Assessment of employee needs, interests, and health risks before offering a program will allow for development of a baseline to which future measurements can be compared. Determination of the number and types of employees who participate in programs, the skills or knowledge gained as a result of participation, and other simple techniques can allow for formative evaluation to occur during the program and for adjustments to be made to ensure success.

- **Process evaluation** metrics could include the number and types of health education events held, the number of employees participating in the events, and the number of calls or requests for more information.

- **Impact evaluation** metrics could include the number and types of fitness classes held, the number of participants in the classes, pre- and post-health assessment information, or the type of policies or system changes supporting the program that were made in the organization.

- **Outcome evaluation** metrics should include a comparison between the organization's healthcare costs versus medical claims trend for both the specific industry vertical and the national medical trend for the year, the number of employees showing a reduction in medical risk conditions, reductions of absenteeism (year over year) and improvements in morale which can be measured through surveys.

Program Categories

Most programs will be targeted at one or more of the following three levels: Awareness, Lifestyle Change, and Supportive Environment. The program plan should identify activities from all three levels to be considered a comprehensive program.

1. **Awareness programs** increase the employees' level of awareness or interest in the topic of the program. Such programs often result in increased knowledge about healthy behavior and can be effective morale boosters and ways to publicize the program to a large number of employees. These types of activities are also an inexpensive way to begin the program.

   Examples: newsletters, posters, health fairs, one-time education classes, brown bag lunch seminars, health screening.

2. **Lifestyle Change programs** are intended to change the health behavior of the employee. Health education and behavior modification are two common methods. Such programs should continue for at least eight to twelve weeks if they are to have any long-term impact.

   Examples: ongoing fitness classes, tobacco cessation, regular meetings of weight-loss groups, extended stress management education

3. **Supportive Environment programs** are intended to create an environment that encourages healthy lifestyles. The major elements of that environment

are the physical setting, departmental policies and culture, ongoing programs and structure, and employee involvement in programs.

Examples: a fitness policy, a "no tobacco" policy, ergonomically friendly environment, healthy food-stocked vending machines

If physical activity is part of an organization's program plan, the organization should consider having all employees who wish to participate first complete a physical fitness readiness questionnaire. This questionnaire will help determine which employees require consultation with a physician before beginning an exercise program. Further, all employees participating in such vigorous physical activity should have signed a statement of informed consent. The legal department of the organization should be consulted for the wording and format of forms to be used.

Program Costs

A budget should be developed that outlines the approximate costs for implementing such a program. The budget should be proposed to the organization's leadership team to identify what is required to carry out the organization's employee wellness program, and it should be reflected in that organization's business plan.

The following areas should be considered in the budget outline when determining the costs of the program:

- Biometric screening, staffing of professional medical personnel, logistics and coordination

- Personnel and/or training costs, including having staff members trained as leaders or instructors of health/fitness education activities

- Buying incentives and awards for employees who participate in an organization's employee wellness program, possibly including award ribbons, certificates, T-shirts, and other low-cost items of recognition

- Paying for employee memberships in a health club or equivalent

- Paying the registration fees to enter teams in sports leagues, 5Ks, and corporate runs

- Buying uniforms or other apparel for an organization's sports teams

- On-site medical screening services (lipid panels) or preventive services (flu shots)

- Any other employee medical support costs, such as portable blood pressure monitoring machines

The concept of cost-sharing has been found to result in a high degree of commitment by those sharing in the cost. An organization may choose to cover 100 percent of the costs of certain program activities, to share the costs of some activities with participating employees, or to have employees pay 100 percent of the costs associated with certain program activities. Cost-sharing should be addressed in the plan.

Program Scheduling

Program activities may be scheduled before, during, between, or after normal working hours, as deemed appropriate by the organization's Leadership team.

Program Coordination

A successful employee wellness program will require appropriate planning, coordination, and implementation. An organization wishing to have such a program will designate an employee wellness coordinator, who would devote on-duty time to the effort. It is unlikely that a successful program can be administered on a strictly volunteer basis after working hours.

Organizations may want to seek opportunities to enter into agreements with other entities in the area that offer access to health education or fitness activity programs. Such cooperation will be particularly useful when services cannot be offered at the worksite.

The following review checklist can be used by the organization to determine the extent to which the plan has identified the health needs of the employees and has systematically reviewed program activity options that will help it to successfully improve the health and well-being of those employees and that of the organization.

1. PROGRAM PURPOSE	YES	NO
a. Description of program purpose		
2. PROGRAM OBJECTIVES	YES	NO
a. Primary goal stated		
b. Measurable objectives stated		
c. Evidence of employee needs, interests considered in planning		
• Awareness activities		
• Lifestyle change activities		
• Supportive environment activities		
• Equipment/supplies		
• Staff instructor training		
• Incentives/awards		
• Memberships in health clubs		
• Sports league/team registration		
• Medical treatment services		
3. ELIGIBILITY REQUIREMENTS	YES	NO
a. All employees eligible		
b. Family members eligible		
4. PROGRAM SCHEDULING	YES	NO
a. Statement of schedule		
5. USE OF FACILITIES	YES	NO
a. Facilities available for use are described		
6. PROVIDERS OF INSTRUCTION/SERVICES	YES	NO
a. Providers' qualifications described		

	YES	NO
7. PROGRAM COORDINATION	YES	NO
a. Wellness coordinator designated		
b. Evidence of attempts at coordination with other programs and services in the area		
	YES	NO
8. FITNESS PROVIDERS MEET QUALIFICATIONS OUTLINED IN THESE SECTIONS		
9. EXPECTED RESULTS	YES	NO
a. Statement of expected results		
b. Expected results conform to objectives		
10. PROGRAM CONTENT	YES	NO
a. Formal activities relate to program objectives and purposes		
b. Evaluation methods described are appropriate to stated program objectives		
11. FORMAL ACTIVITIES LISTED UNDER	YES	NO
a. Awareness		
b. Lifestyle change		
c. Supportive environment		
	YES	NO
12. EMPLOYEE PARTICIPATION IN ON-SITE PROGRAMS OR SCREENING IS ADDRESSED		
13. LEGAL		
14. PROGRAM COSTS	YES	NO
a. Budget outline prepared		
b. Source of funds identified		
c. Costs are considered for		
• Facilites modification		
• Providers of instruction/services		

YEAR TWO:
EDUCATION AND INCENTIVES

The next stage of the program is the educational component. Once employees know their numbers and understand their problem areas, then they can take advantage of the various programs we put together. For example, if an employee discovers through the screening that he has diabetes or a heart condition, then he can focus in on those program components that deliver information for him to better control his condition.

As the program becomes more entrenched in the company, some employers begin rewards programs that include incentives for those employees who are actively participating. On the flip side, those employees who choose not to participate will see their choices reflected in their premiums. Again, 80 percent of claims come from chronic illnesses that are controllable, yet there are people out there who choose not to participate in helping to reduce and stabilize healthcare costs.

The paradigm shift is about employers and employees seeing how they can be part of the solution to control healthcare costs. If your organization can continue to get employees to shift their thinking about wellness as a benefit as opposed to sick care, you can also improve corporate culture and employee engagement in other aspects of your business as well as the bottom line.

By demonstrating to employees an attitude of responsibility—for employees, for clients, for your industry, and for the business itself—you'll begin to cultivate and attract better-quality employees. According to a recent study conducted by MetLife, 73 percent of participants of corporate wellness programs feel that by offering such programs, employers are demonstrating that they care about their workforces' well-being.[1]

Those employees that buy into the idea of well care over sick care will also become some of your most engaged employees. They understand that whatever they do impacts the business because employees can affect a business either favorably or unfavorably. What we're trying to do is to have more employees affect businesses in a favorable manner, and we want to reward them for that.

Most employees have a payroll deduction that goes toward their health insurance premiums. As part of changing mind-sets, those employees who believe in wellness start to question why their premiums are also paying for those people who have unhealthy habits like smoking or not exercising: in short, people who don't want to take care of themselves and are not willing to be part of the solution.

It was written into the ACA legislation that employers can provide a 30 percent reduction to the payroll deduction for healthcare for employees who participate in wellness programs. That's an incredible incentive for employees to be part of the solution. That 30 percent reduction in their payroll deduction costs the employer very little, but the effect on claims is huge. For very few dollars (the reduction in premium for the employee) the effect these wellness programs have on claims can convert into hundreds of thousands—and sometimes millions of dollars—in savings for the employer's bottom line.

CASE STUDY: INCENTIVES BOOST WELLNESS PARTICIPATION AT A LARGE HEALTHCARE ORGANIZATION

Sapoznik Insurance worked with a large healthcare organization with 2,500 employees in acute care hospitals spread across the country.

Interestingly, even though this group of people are in the healthcare industry, we found a surprising lack of attention being paid to their own nutritional and health needs. Nurses, for example, worked very long shifts, often had irregular hours (which tend to disrupt sleep), and had eating habits that promoted unhealthy food choices.

At the onset of our relationship with the group, we found elevated levels of hypertension, obesity, and other serious, preventable, and reversible illnesses. In a three year period, coinciding with the deployment of our wellness program, this client's combined medical services per member per month costs (PMPM) were improving when compared against the national benchmark average for all industries as well as that of the healthcare services industry.

In 2013, the national claims average for all industries was $252.83 per member per month.

Surprisingly to some, claims in the healthcare industry, (e.g. employees of hospitals, urgent care centers, clinics) are higher than the national average. The healthcare industry claims average was $267.96 PMPM.

After year 3 of our wellness program, our client's PMPM claims costs were $225.88 PMPM.

The group outperformed both the industry and national averages by 16% and 11% respectively, having a significant impact on their bottom line.

This translated into a combined realized savings of nearly $1.8 million when compared against other health service organizations. In three years, we were able to reverse the overall trend of unhealthiness and change the culture to one of wellness.

We were able to do this by linking wellness programs to a payroll deduction strategy—participants in the program received a discount toward their health insurance premiums. We experienced a 75 percent participation rate in medical screenings, which gave us the ability to disseminate valuable information about preventive care. By revealing to individuals that they had conditions such as hypertension, diabetes or obesity, we were able to help them learn to correct or control problems through lifestyle changes and medication.

In addition to biometric screenings, activities we implemented for the group included medication reminder apps and "lunch-and-learns" to help participants under-stand how to prepare meals for work rather than using the snack machine. We also altered cafeteria and vending machine options to include healthier choices and subsi-dized vending machine bottled water to make it a more appealing choice than costlier soft drinks.

By tracking results, the organization noticed that there was an increase in preventive health visits. As a result, there was a decrease in the number of costly medical claims incurred by employees. This demonstrates a cor-relation between preventive care and reduced number of claims. When the number of serious claims decrease, the organization benefits from better health insurance rates.

Without incentives, employee participation in voluntary wellness programs is typically in the 15 to 20 percent range. But there is a huge shift in participation when incentives are offered to employees in the form of a reduction to their payroll deduction for healthcare premiums.

As soon as we introduce on-site biometric screenings and organize incentive programs, we normally see that 15 to 20 percent employee participation rate increases to as much as 96 percent, with a median of around 80 percent participation with a well-organized, incentive-based wellness program. As an employer, when you have 80 to 96 percent of your employees participating in a wellness program, you can be certain that your healthcare costs and your claims costs are going to decrease substantially.

YEAR THREE:
MEASURING RESULTS

Although results are measured every year of the program, typically some of the most notable results are seen around the three-year mark. Data is gathered starting in year one and through each subsequent year of the wellness program. By year three, the data gathered becomes much more meaningful because the data is coming from employees who have adapted their behavior based on the education and incentives they've received. By now, your organization will have made strides positively influencing healthier lifestyles and behaviors. There are numerous local and national associations that showcase employers who are making a difference. Make it a priority to share your success story with others and build enthusiasm while gaining additional momentum for next year. Through these efforts, you might very well be recognized as the next Healthiest Employer in your industry.

In year three, we continue measuring results against your own baseline and against those of the organization and your peer groups. For instance, participating employees that were made aware in year one that they had very high blood pressure would have visited their physicians, obtained prescriptions, and taken medications to lower their numbers. By years two and three, the aggregate data would demonstrate a significant decrease in blood pressure, reflecting the consistent use of medication and participation in the wellness programs. These employees took real steps to manage their condition and are seeing results through better health.

In year three, employees can participate in self-directed activities and manage their participation through a personal portal. The activities they participate in earn reward points, and points can be used to purchase exercise equipment, bicycles, wearable devices, activity trackers, movie tickets, and even a seven-day vacation. In addition to better health and lower premiums, there are some real, tangible rewards at this stage of the program.

In this stage of the program, employers often partner with fitness facilities to offer gym memberships, exercise classes, CPR training, and more.

Although not permitted to see employees' health information or records, due to HIPAA regulations, employers are allowed to see participation statistics that show them how many employees are moving from being sedentary to more engaged participants. The employers can also see the impact of participation on the employees, and the program itself can begin to build on successes and evolve with employees' changing needs.

Again, the goal of the program is to be flexible and agile. The real goal is to get started, and then develop the program with the employer's input. Every industry is a little different, and each employer has different dynamics. We start with the framework of the program, and then we work closely with employers to develop customized programs that work for them. We have modules that make it easy for employers to tailor their programs to meet their employees' unique needs.

BEYOND YEAR THREE
COMPARING PERFORMANCE

The goal moving forward is to evaluate and continuously improve. To do this, we continue to improve the initiatives that are working well by keeping them fresh and original, while also modifying the ones that are not showing results. While working with our clients, we also open up access to experts in the space of health and wellness by attending local, regional, or even national conferences to learn about best practices. Ongoing, continuing education is key for us and our clients.

At this point in the wellness program, wellness is ingrained in the company culture, and we really start seeing the passion for wellness grow. Each year, before they can receive discounts on their health-care premium payroll deductions, employees must complete their biometric screening and a personal health risk assessment. Measurements now include a year-over-year comparison of participation and performance. The activities listed below provide opportunities for employers to continue fostering a passion for wellness.

1. Educate Employees with Health-Related Campaigns

Use every opportunity that a wellness program affords to educate and inspire employees to take control of their health. Choose monthly wellness campaigns that educate employees about their personal health goals.

A great way to make a wellness program work for all employees is to offer free, quarterly healthy lunches for employees. If you have a cafeteria or break rooms on-site, use these spaces to teach about healthy cooking and offer food choices that are healthy and low in fat. The impact that some of the recipes highlighted in a cooking class will have on the company's bottom line is well worth the small budget it takes to organize such an event.

2. Host Wellness Practitioner Events

In every community, there are many wellness providers to be found. Search them out, and partner with them to speak to your employees at wellness events. Invite a healthy lifestyle coach to teach meditation, or have massage therapists offer chair massages in a meeting room at your business.

3. Continue to Offer On-Site Wellness Screenings

Along with your wellness fair, give employees a chance to get their biometric data checked. A corporate occupational health provider or local urgent care clinic can send qualified nurses to conduct tests for blood pressure, weight/height measurements, and blood levels. They can also administer the flu shots for your employees.

4. Offer Flu Shots for Free

As mentioned above, flu shots help support wellness in the workplace. They can be offered at a low cost to your employees by contracting with a local occupational health center or by offering to pay for flu shots at a nearby pharmacy.

5. Make Stress a Thing of the Past

As much as possible, create an atmosphere and activities that focus on reducing stress in the workplace. Set up periodic access to chair massage sessions, or make regular yoga and even meditation sessions part of your corporate culture. These efforts alone can help make your corporate wellness program a long-term success with all team members.

Incorporating these action steps in the following years and keep your wellness program from becoming stale and predictable. The key is to keep employees engaged by sharing positive testimonials and encouraging feedback at every turn. Tell these stories and post anecdotes throughout your organization—on your intranet, on posters or as short videos. Remember, the goal is to replicate these positive behaviors so that they permeate throughout the organization and promote a healthier lifestyle.

INFLUENCING CORPORATE CULTURE

By implementing all of the steps discussed above, employers typically see significant shifts in their company's culture. The Best Practices Scorecard is introduced and used to guide development of the strategic plan. The Scorecard is viewed as a roadmap for the Sapoznik 3-Year Worksite Wellness Plan because foundational elements of comprehensive, science-based employee wellness programs are used. The Scorecard's core elements are strategic planning, leadership engagement, program management and engagement, and evaluation and measurement. Recommended guidelines provide suggestions for effectively addressing physical activity, nutrition, and obesity.

The Sapoznik 3-Year Worksite Wellness Plan showcases essential collaborative partners, key activities over three years, and their connection to the intended outcomes of better health for employees and their respective families.

The annual and semiannual progress reports we generate show data from health assessments and biometric screenings. The reports highlight accomplishments and areas to improve, continue, or eliminate throughout the plan. As your company makes this journey, it expands its horizons. But all of this comes through a multiyear evolution; a successful program doesn't happen by implementing all of these pieces at the same time. They must be implemented strategically in order to achieve lasting results.

STRATEGIES FOR COMMUNICATING YOUR WELLNESS PLAN

COMBINING TRADITIONAL COMMUNICATION WITH INNOVATIVE TECHNOLOGY

Wellness information needs to be communicated through a variety of channels. On the low-tech end, we adorn the workplace with messaging through inspirational posters that suggest healthier eating, meditation, and exercise. These are placed in strategic areas, like elevators and stairwells, where employees see them every day, to encourage them to make better choices.

Using modern technology, we're able to introduce some very innovative program features. For instance, we are now introducing companies to the idea of telehealth. The concept of telehealth has been around since the mid-1960s, but it has only recently come into its own, as technology and regulations have made it more accessible to all consumers. Telehealth was first conceived as a way to provide healthcare services to underserved rural areas. It was strictly a doctor-to-doctor or doctor-to-nurse consultation, by either phone or dedicated video connection.

We are also using technology in other innovative ways. For example, we suggest sending text and e-mail reminders to employees to participate in and be compliant with the wellness program. There are also applications today that allow you to measure your heart rate with your smartphone. There is also technology that informs families of a diabetic's noncompliance, alerting them if a diabetic person has not had his or her glucose test that day.

Online programs also help with chronic illness, such as a two-minute breathing program that can be done at a person's desk to help reduce stress. The program, which is available as an app on a smartphone, can bring down stress levels.

When mixing technology and healthcare information, it's important for employees to understand that their health information is protected by the HIPAA laws. Employers have no access to the actual information; they only know how many of their employees are participating in programs. The information is there for the employees, to help them become healthy and to maintain that level of health so that the employer can provide them with affordable healthcare and they can enjoy the benefits of a healthier lifestyle.

By communicating through a variety of means, we're able to reach employees where, when, and how they need to receive information, thereby removing barriers to nonparticipation. Today, employers want programs brought to them; we make it simple and accessible for them. We're trying to remove all the obstacles and all the excuses to make it as easy as possible for employees to participate. For example, not being able to get to the gym is no excuse: through technology, we're able to bring workout programs to employees. One company we've partnered with provides entire yoga and fitness workout routines that can be run off of any mobile device from virtually anywhere.

Whether they are traveling or are away from their local gym, technology is now allowing people to access wellness and get motivated like never before. The digital future—along with the gamification of wellness—will bring us an even brighter tomorrow.

ADOPTION ACROSS GENERATIONS

It's well documented that there are differences between generations in the workplace; depending on the demographic, people receive and interpret information differently. Generational differences call for different methods of communication. That's why we use a multi-channel, multitiered approach to more effectively deliver the message of wellness to everyone in the workplace.

This Differences in the Workplace chart (next page) gives you a good idea of how vastly diverse our workforce is today, because we are in a transition. We're moving away from the traditionalists, who had very little exposure to computers and technology as they grew up, to the millennials, who use technology as a primary method of communication.

As employers, it's important to be aware that the demographics represented in this chart communicate via different methods; in essence, they speak different languages. Those different languages are very important in understanding how to communicate, and communication is the key to any good wellness program.

	TRADITIONALISTS	BABY BOOMERS	GENERATION X	MILLENNIALS
OUTLOOK	Practical	Optimistic	Skeptical, individualistic	Hopeful and optimistic
WORK ETHIC	Loyal, sacrifice	Driven	Balanced	Eager but anxious
VALUE IN WORK-PLACE	Similarity (melting pot)	Profitability, reputation	Stimulation, autonomy	Diversity, structure, relationships
VIEWS ON AUTHORITY	Chain of com-mand	Change of command	Self-command	Don't command-collaborate
VIEWS ON LEAD-ERSHIP	By hierarchy	By consensus	By competency	By pulling together
FEEDBACK	No news is good news	Once a year with documentation	Periodic with 360 degrees	Impersonal at touch of button
TIME AT WORK IS DEFINED AS	Punch clock	Visibility	Why does it matter if I get it done at 2 am?	Is it 5 pm? I have a life.
COMMUNICATION	Formal (Memo) or face-to-face	Telephone	Email	IM/Texting, social networking
PREFERRED LEARNING METHOD	Expert	Expert	From each other	Group, interactive, technology
MOTIVATED BY	Respect for experience	Achievement	Do it your way	Collaboration

The US Bureau of Labor Statistics predicts that 2015 is the year that millennials will make up the majority of the workforce, and that proportion is expected to rise to 75 percent by 2030.[2] Hiring, engaging, and retaining this demographic will require a different approach in the workplace. According to PricewaterhouseCoopers:

> Some experts believe that healthcare benefits have less influence on employee recruitment and retention post-ACA because insurance exchanges provide non-employer based health insurance options.

Innovators will look beyond traditional health benefits and support more engaging and supportive end-to-end employee experiences, with a greater focus on how the employee experience influences the overall well-being and engagement of that worker...

Insurers and healthcare organizations will work closely with employers and consumers to support and enhance the well-being of their members and patients. They will work to understand and deliver on the expectations of this new generation of millennials[3].

Millennials love the Internet: they grew up with it, they understand it, and they prefer to communicate using it. So when we're trying to communicate with millennials about activities and other program information, we use text messages, the Internet, Twitter, and other social media channels.

But the baby boomer generation, which still makes up a very large percentage of our workforce, tends to prefer physical forms of communication. Boomers prefer more on-site information and sometimes require more in-person coaching.

That's why, when designing a wellness program, it's important that we take into consideration the different types of employees in your workplace. We put together programs that speak to all generations—millennials, Gen X, and baby boomers. The result is a program that is much broader in scope.

Because of the generational differences, we don't take a one-size-fits-all approach to educating people about wellness. We want employers to move away from the thought that everybody's going to be online, that everyone will meet on-site, or that everyone needs a printed booklet to read. We deliver the education component of our program by using a broad spectrum of choices because we have three employee groups (the millennials, Gen X, and the baby boomers) in one workplace today, and each of them need to be communicated with differently.

Think about this: the year 2030 is not very far away, and if 75 percent of the workforce at that point will be millennials, then those are the people who are going to be running our companies. We need to learn and understand now how to communicate with tomorrow's leaders.

Despite their differences, there are some similarities between the demographics. Boomers are very interested in the quality of the care, and according to an August 2012 Google/Nielsen Boomer Survey, 78 percent of baby boomers research online for health information about treatments, medication side effects, ratings, and reviews after seeing an advertisement or information on television.[4] Their online searches also target information for their parents and their children.

According to the survey, Gen Xers also search online for ratings and reviews, but they are quicker than boomers to switch providers based on a recent experience: a trait they share with millennials. As with the other groups, millennials also search online for information; however, in addition to advertising and online reviews, they are also heavily influenced by social networks. Boomers are much more inclined to go with verbal referrals from someone they know or someone a friend knows.

So on the subject of wellness communication, boomers are better served by a combination of services. When we're putting our wellness plan together, we're talking to the boomers and coaching them through the process. With millennials, we're using the Internet and technology to try to communicate with them about the benefits of being healthy.

Whatever the preference, we're using all forms of communication to encourage employees to participate, and we're allowing them to naturally gravitate toward the form of communication that they prefer. Whether it's a text message, e-mail, Facebook, on-site material, or some other means of communication, we've addressed the generational preferences.

We send out e-mail newsletters to individuals who request them. We tweet short, concise suggestions and information about wellness on a daily basis. We post on our Facebook page and on the employer's Facebook page. We bring in on-site professionals to talk about wellness issues ranging from heart health to diabetes to breast and prostate cancer awareness. We also offer online videos, which is a great way to communicate across the generations.

We're constantly evolving our methods, because we recognize that what works today may not work tomorrow. In fifteen years, the PDF newsletter may be gone; social apps similar to Twitter might become the standard communication method as attention spans continue to shrink.

WELLNESS BLUEPRINT SUMMARY

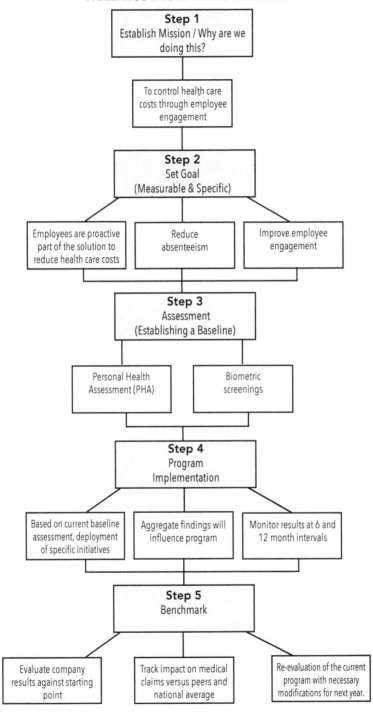

Step 1
Establish Mission / Why are we doing this?

To control health care costs through employee engagement

Step 2
Set Goal
(Measurable & Specific)

Employees are proactive part of the solution to reduce health care costs

Reduce absenteeism

Improve employee engagement

Step 3
Assessment
(Establishing a Baseline)

Personal Health Assessment (PHA)

Biometric screenings

Step 4
Program Implementation

Based on current baseline assessment, deployment of specific initiatives

Aggregate findings will influence program

Monitor results at 6 and 12 month intervals

Step 5
Benchmark

Evaluate company results against starting point

Track impact on medical claims versus peers and national average

Re-evaluation of the current program with necessary modifications for next year.

1 Boston College Center for Work & Family, "The MetLife Study of Financial Wellness Across the Globe: A Look at How Multinational Companies Are Helping Employees Better Manage Their Personal Finances," MetLife, 2011, accessed July 25, 2015, https://www.metlife.com/assets/institutional/products/benefits-products/ml-global-financial-wellness-study.pdf.

2 Alistair Mitchell, "The Rise of the Millennial Workforce," Wired, accessed March 23, 2015, http://www.wired.com/2013/08/the-rise-of-the-millennial-workforce/.

3 "Issue 9: Redefining health and well-being for the millennial generation," PwC, http://www.pwc.com/us/en/health-industries/top-health-industry-issues/millennials.html.

4 Smitha Gopal, "Healthcare Decisions by Generation: How Do Patients Differ?" Eyemaginations, November 6, 2014, http://blog.eyemaginations.com/healthcare-decisions-generation-patients-differ/.

CHAPTER 6

A CULTURE SHIFT

Wellness programs are changing the way employees view employers in a positive way, and the result is a sense of loyalty, increased employee engagement, improved productivity, and a more profitable bottom line.

A wellness program means a new outlook for a company; it's more than just a program touting better eating and exercise. It's a complete culture shift: a call to action that now is the time to see life through a different lens. It's the difference between a drab, dingy stairwell no one ever uses and a brightly painted stairwell adorned with posters meant to inspire healthier living. Who wants to be in a dark stairwell? A simple activity like spending a few dollars to paint a stairwell increases the number of people using it exponentially.

By bringing in a wellness program, we change the way that you and your company as a whole think about healthcare. We do more than just bring in a few new programs; we transform perceptions and behaviors to create something truly sustainable. We inspire people to change—to have a lifelong passion for wellness.

As we discussed in chapter 5, *The Wellness Program Blueprint*, in the early stages of the program, we form a wellness team led by influential employees who work within the strategy that we put together to motivate and stimulate a competitive, yet fun, environment. Then we integrate the strategy with existing programs for employees, and we also bring in new services as we progress through the program. These include innovative services that employees may have never had access to in the past and that are designed to get employees engaged.

We examine the data that we collect from the biometric screenings, and we determine what percentage of the employees are smokers or diabetic, how many people have heart disease or are overweight, and the prevalence of other conditions. Once we have all of those general statistics, we build and blend programs to make the idea of wellness interesting and fun. Through these programs, we can develop measures for determining results, and we can begin to influence change.

The measurements we gather throughout the program help us develop a roadmap to guide us as we integrate wellness into the culture at work. This is not a one-shot deal; it is a total integration into the work environment that is created as we embark on the strategy of stabilizing healthcare costs. That's our ultimate goal: we are trying to reduce healthcare costs, increase productivity, reduce absenteeism, and create a culture shift within the organization.

A PICTURE OF THE ORGANIZATION AFTER THE PROGRAM

Once the organization is on their wellness journey, it is no longer reactive when it comes to healthcare. Now, the organization is proactive; it is passionate about wellness, and its view of healthcare is upbeat, positive, and forward-thinking. People no longer think about their healthcare benefit as a way to take care of them when they're sick; they view it as a resource for helping them to stay healthy.

At the beginning of this book, we talked about what a reactive organization looks like: It's combating rising healthcare costs from emergency room visits that cost thousands of dollars. People are having catastrophic claims for strokes, cancers, heart attacks, and other preventable diseases. The organization is experiencing high deductibles, and healthcare costs are out of control. It's continually changing plans, which means that employees are continually changing providers. Employees are missing work, and there is high turnover. And those who do come to work engage in behaviors that lead to poor health: they smoke, they're overweight, and sometimes they come to work with an illness.

This is an organization that can't figure out why it is having so many problems containing healthcare costs. It's a company that hasn't figured out that those problems are arising from the fact that it just hasn't gotten its healthcare act together.

Now let's picture that same organization post-wellness program. What does it look like? It's a company that is able to identify at-risk workers and is better able to pinpoint problems before they lead to high healthcare costs. This is a company that is promoting wellness and moving into a position to proactively manage wellness and to change the dynamics of healthcare. The employer has been able to get employees so well organized that, where its healthcare costs are concerned, the company is properly managed.

A company who has successfully implemented a wellness program is one that is working more on the preventive end and is not just reacting to high-cost claims that can drive up rates. For example, consider those employees who, because of genetics, have a propensity toward high blood pressure, diabetes, or obesity. After three years, those employees will be the ones who will reap the benefits, because your organization has helped them address their risk factors. Because of the programs you have implemented in the workplace, those employees have been educated as to how they can control the chronic illnesses they may be genetically predisposed to.

Now you're looking at a company where people are not sedentary: employees are moving around and finding ways to be active while working. There are organized activities, people are achieving goals, and there is a true mission statement regarding good health.

This is a place where people are happier; they're smiling because they feel better and they're healthier. The problems that existed with healthcare and its costs are no longer an unknown part of the company's bottom line. Healthcare costs are under control, and employees have the tools they need to work through any issues that they have. Employees have more avenues for finding answers when they have a health question because there is an organized process for them to follow, the answers are made readily available through a variety of methods, and the entire program has followed a well-defined roadmap.

This is a place where people want to come to work. One of the greatest achievements many companies experience is being an employer of choice—of being a place where people love to work. So now absenteeism and turnover has been drastically reduced and those positions that do come open are easily filled by a waiting list of interested, qualified candidates.

The effects of the program also go beyond the walls of the company, with employees taking their new knowledge home to their families. Now you have workers whose families, relatives, and friends are also happier and healthier. Without the burden of unhealthy family members to care or pay for, your employees are able to focus more on the tasks at hand when they are at work. As a result, productivity has skyrocketed. Employees are producing more, not only because they can but also because they want to. And the work they're producing is of far better quality.

THE BENEFITS OF WELLNESS

Twenty-six of the companies that have participated in our program have statistics showing that, year after year, their healthcare premiums are approximately 17 percent lower than those of their peer organizations. This is backed by Florida Blue's Health Plan Performance Report, which compiles statistics based on the group's performance after having implemented wellness programs and ranks its performance against that of companies in different vertical markets and against industry peers.

We've also seen employers with wellness programs experience a 19 percent reduction of absenteeism. Employees who participate are going to be healthier, so workers' compensation claims are reduced along with incidences of heart attack, stroke, and other illnesses, which can lead to higher premiums based on catastrophic and long-term disability claims.

With the median age of today's American workers at forty-two years and four months, they're at the point in their lives where they are prone to serious illness or accident.[1] What we've found is that employees working in companies with organized wellness programs are in better shape when they come to work, so they're better able to avoid workplace injuries.

That's good news because when an employee is out on a long-term disability claim it is not just the employee that is affected. The employer has to replace that employee, and the person taking that employee's place may not have the knowledge or depth of insight into the job that the seasoned employee had. Not only is the employer paying out a disability claim, but he's also losing productivity while getting the replacement employee up to speed. And it's the same with workers' compensation and catastrophic claims.

Wellness programs simply make for a happier workforce. Today's generations are not just looking for monetary compensation; they're looking for work-life balance. And part of that balance comes from working in an environment that promotes physical and mental health and that respects the fact that the employee is an integral part of the business. Employees who feel wanted tend to give employers all they've got because they know they are part of a bigger picture.

In fact, a wellness program is a big differentiator for companies today. A study done by Principal Financial found that 45 percent of Americans in small and midsize companies say that they would stay in their jobs longer because of an employer-sponsored wellness program.[2] The study found that some workers said they were encouraged to work harder and perform better, and there was a 26 percent drop in the number of missed days simply by implementing a workplace wellness program.

GREATER STABILITY

Overall, a wellness program stabilizes your healthcare costs. This means that you, the employer, don't have to change carriers because premiums got so high that your employees can no longer afford the insurance. All that does is make for an unsettling environment that doesn't attract employees. What does it mean when employees have to move to another carrier? It may mean changing doctors, changing pediatricians, and changing specialists. So stabilizing the premium structure is also about stabilizing the overall plan, which gives employees the consistency of using the same doctors and prevents possible gaps in knowledge between providers when employees have to change from one to another simply because of higher premiums.

It used to be that healthcare costs were done in a vacuum; the human resource department just dished out benefits at rates that were set until next year. Well that doesn't work anymore. We're changing the way healthcare costs are perceived by making consumerism an integral part of today's workplace culture. Consumerism is a movement that advocates patients' involvement in their own healthcare decisions. We want employees to know that they must be part of the solution if we're going to rein in costs. For employees, the biggest rewards are that they feel, act, and work healthier, and their employers have healthier workplaces that reduce healthcare costs and remain profitable.

1   "Labor Force Statistics from the Current Population Survey," US Bureau of Labor Statistics, accessed July 26, 2015, http://www.bls.gov/cps/occupation_age.htm.

2   Lisa Welshhons, "How Employee Wellness Programs Can Generate Savings for Your Company," Merit Resources, accessed July 26, 2015, http://www.meritresoaurces.com/userdocs/materials/Employee_Wellness_Initiatives_Merit.pdf.

CHAPTER 7

THE IMPACT BEYOND THE OFFICE

O nce the employer introduces the idea of wellness at work, the wellness concept is likely to disseminate to the entire family and ultimately spread into the community. As the saying goes, "It takes a village to raise a child." To that, I'd like to add,

"IT TAKES A COMMUNITY TO MAKE A HEALTHY ENVIRONMENT."

Every one of us is responsible for that community. From our workplace and our employees to our parents and our schools, we all have to work together because we will all benefit from this.

What are you doing as an organization? Where do you need to really make a change? When—and how quickly—can change start?

I believe that another place to start is with our children. By taking responsibility for having healthier kids, we're going to have fewer medical issues in the future.

OUR CHILDREN—THE FUTURE CONSUMERS OF HEALTHCARE

At Sapoznik Insurance, we participate in a variety of activities that promote and foster healthier communities. One of the activities we're involved in is the championing of food gardens for elementary schools in the Miami area.

We're working with The Education Fund, an organization that works with public schools in South Florida to enhance cultural awareness through art, music, and developing an interest in the overall well-being of the student. Together, we've worked to develop the Edible Gardens campaign, which teaches children about better eating (literally from the ground up) by designing gardens in elementary schools that are cultivated by the schoolchildren themselves.

TRANSFORMING THE TRADITIONAL CLASSROOM

Through a grant from The Education Fund, Twin Lakes Elementary School in Hialeah, Florida, has transformed the traditional classroom. Although the school was high-performing, it saw that students were trapped in the classroom for the majority of the day, which led to low motivation and stress for teachers.

The school used grant money to start a garden and involved students and teachers in the project. In time, the gardens expanded and grew until they were well beyond the original plans. Students harvest the fruits and vegetables themselves, and the school's cafeteria then prepares the food and serves it to students. The garden has also been integrated into every subject area, from science to math to art.

Today, the school is planning to expand the garden in a sustainable way, and it is working to create one of the nation's early elementary school-based permaculture food forests. By maximizing its resources, the school hopes to one day grow enough crops to provide a large portion of the school cafeteria's produce.[1]

Through these gardens, children are learning about fruits, vegetables, and better eating options. They are actually planting the produce—such as carrots, kale, lettuce, and eggplant—while sharing this newfound passion with their families. Children are supplied with easy and fun-to-make recipes for chopped salads and simple snacks that they are encouraged to prepare at home. Surprisingly, the children had never before seen many of the fresh fruits and vegetables that they are growing! By helping these children learn how to grow the produce and making it possible for them to eat these fresh items, we are developing their palates along with an understanding of a balanced diet. The principals of the schools are working very closely with our programs so that when the children harvest the produce and herbs, they are being integrated into the lunch programs and into the water that the children drink. For example, rosemary is being used on cheese sandwiches, water is infused with basil, and tomatoes are being used on sandwiches and salads.

The kids get so excited about the gardens they are building that they are starting to incorporate the foods into their own lives by sharing with siblings and, of course, parents. As we teach the children, they then teach their parents. Kids teaching their parents about nutrition is helping to reverse the disconnect from nutrition that comes from generations of supersizing. When a child comes home and declares that she doesn't want to eat junk food and instead wants to make popsicles out of watermelon juice from fruit that she helped grow, then we feel that we're starting to influence change. These kids are actually putting incredible emphasis on this—it's a beautiful thing.

Within our community, we must help our children understand nutrition. Even corporate America has joined in the cause; they're helping us build these gardens so that the children can then become healthier, more productive people in our society. In fact, in 2015, The Education Fund received a grant from Citibank for $400,000 to help continue to grow these gardens because there's such energy behind the project. This grant was part of an initiative aimed squarely at influencing how children and the next generation eat and exercise as we tackle epidemics like childhood obesity.

The alternative to projects like these community gardens is to do nothing and to accept our society as is. Right now, one in three children between the ages of two and nineteen is overweight or obese. In Dade County, Florida, alone, 33 percent of children under age eighteen are either borderline or fully diabetic.[2]

As we have stated throughout the book, think about those numbers: If they are in those categories today as children, what will their numbers look like as adults? What does that mean for our future?

Think about the cost of caring for diabetes and other diseases and conditions: How will those costs be managed in the future if the nation continues to foster an environment that promotes rather than prevents diabetes? How high are healthcare costs going to skyrocket? What will society have to sacrifice to pay for burgeoning healthcare costs in the future? Education, infrastructure, or other things? There will not be enough money to deal with all the illnesses if we don't start making a difference today.

Starting today, as responsible community businesses, we can make a difference in our local school systems. To me, the school system (along with the workplace) is one of the best places to start educating individuals about wellness and nutrition. We are using that system to help educate children, who help educate the parents. We are looking at it from multiple angles—the schools, the workplace, having kids educate parents, and having parents take home what they've learned in their workplaces—to really get the word out that promoting good health is important to all of us.

We have an opportunity to really make a difference with these kids and help them educate themselves about nutrition. One of the biggest disservices to our children is not fully educating them about what nutrition should mean to them and our community. This is one of the reasons why we are seeing chronic diseases at levels we've never before seen in the history of the United States.

The time has come. The pendulum has swung. It's time that we all take responsibility for learning about proper nutrition; it's time to change our future.

HEALTHY FAMILIES, HEALTHY BOTTOM LINES

The health of each employee's family also impacts an employer's bottom line. If a child gets sick and has a chronic illness, the cost of care for that child affects the employer's insurance.

But it does more than that. It's not just the employer's insurance. When a parent is taking care of a sick child, they are not at work. It's also likely to impact absenteeism. It's going to impact profitability because even if that employee is at work, he's not really able to concentrate and perform at his best because he has a child at home who is ill.

Part of what we're trying to do is ensure employees understand that employers care about them and want them to be healthy. If we succeed, that information gets shared at home.

Typically, we find that the bad habits of parents have an adverse effect on their children. For example, how many children end up in the emergency room with asthmatic attacks because of a smoking parent? How many children are obese because of the unhealthy eating habits of their parents, who are also obese?

When parents are unhealthy, their kids are likely learning to be unhealthy, and when illness sets in, everyone is affected. Children, whose immune systems are not yet strong, get sick because of unhealthy learned behaviors, and then they miss school, the parent misses work—it's a snowball effect. We help people see the connections. These are the things that we, as employers, want to be able to change because it's going to help all of us.

Absenteeism costs a lot of money, so instead of just dealing with absenteeism, employers need to understand the whole dynamic of what's going on and what's causing employees to be away from work. It's one thing to teach an employee the concept of well care over sick care, but there's a much bigger impact if the employee takes the information home to their family and incorporates those changes.

WELLNESS AS A WAY OF LIFE

As Americans, we've had the luxury of living in the greatest country in the world. However, it's time we think about what could be a looming disaster for the United States if we continue spending company resources on healthcare costs instead of innovation.

As employers, what else could you do with all those dollars you're spending on healthcare benefits? If we take the time now to really understand and develop the whole strategy that health and wellness are a way of life, we will start to create a healthier America. A healthier America will be able to use those dollars in incubators to develop technology, rather than in emergency rooms. Instead of using those dollars for prescription drugs because people have so many medical issues, we can use those dollars for creativity, innovation and job creation.

When you consider that there are 350 million Americans, and a large percentage of them today have preventable diseases which we're doing nothing about, what kind of future can we expect?

I say that we can do something about it. There's no better time than right now, because healthcare reform is here. Employers must provide insurance for their employees if they have fifty or more employees. We have to take control of how we educate our employees, our society, and our children on how important it is to stay healthy, be responsible, and take control of their health. That will affect the world that we live in.

Employers are also dealing with what we call the "Sandwich Generation," where one in four families also has to take care of an elderly parent or relative.[3] So, in addition to employees missing work to take care of children, they're also missing work to take care of aging family members. In fact, 57 percent of working caregivers say that they have had to go to work late, leave early, or take time off to provide care for a family member.[4] This happens to employers every day in the workplace; every day, we're dealing with absenteeism and with the effects of those absent employees.

In the years to come, if steps are not taken today to help our sickly children become healthier, then the percent of the workforce that is taking care of ill children is going to disrupt the work environment even more.

Wellness programs are here to help reduce costs, to change behavior, and to increase profitability and sustainability. They're here to make you the best and the brightest in your industry. Wellness programs do take a concerted effort, and they need to create change that affects the entire community. That begins by understanding that we can accept responsibility and make a difference. We must take proactive steps to reduce the epidemic of childhood obesity. We can change the future for children and their health.

Our children are the workforce of tomorrow. The children who are in school today will be applying to work for you tomorrow. You, as an employer, must understand that this is an all-encompassing issue that affects everyone. It affects how much we pay for every single item that we purchase because when healthcare costs are out of control, companies have to increase the pricing of their products and services.

I've said it a number of times: change doesn't happen overnight. If you want your workers of tomorrow to be healthy, then you need to get your employees on board today. Your future profitability is in the hands of your workforce; they will either take you to new heights of innovation and profitability, or they will bring you down and mire you with the heaviness of chronic illnesses. It's time to take control, to take responsibility, and to create a culture of wellness.

1   "Plant a Thousand Gardens Collaborative Nutrition Initiative," The Education Fund, accessed July 26, 2015, http://www.educationfund.org/programs/collaborativenutritioninitiative/.

2   "Statistics about Diabetes," American Diabetes Association, accessed July 26, 2015, http://www.diabetes.org/diabetes-basics/statistics/.

3   "Selected Caregiver Statistics," Family Caregiver Alliance, accessed July 26, 2015, https://caregiver.org/selected-caregiver-statistics.

4   "Caregiving in the US," The National Alliance for Caregiving and AARP, accessed July 26, 2015, http://www.caregiving.org/data/04execsumm.pdf.

CHAPTER 8

THE TIME TO ACT IS NOW

Throughout the book, I've discussed the changing landscape of healthcare and the importance of taking control of your healthcare costs. These spiraling healthcare costs can be mitigated through corporate wellness programs that have been discussed in detail all through the book. As employers, the time to take action is now.

YOU CAN TAKE CONTROL

You can take control if you take the time to educate yourself about a corporate wellness program. In my experience, employers that embrace the idea of wellness in the workplace feel that they are in a better position and have sustainable programs that are more manageable than those employers who choose not to embrace wellness.

You can make a difference in the direction of your company by implementing the four basic principles: educating your employees, having them take responsibility, incentivizing them, and doing it all with passion.

The root of all business is "follow the numbers." Well, healthcare is also about following the numbers. As those numbers improve, there's a direct correlation with lower absenteeism, higher satisfaction, and better results, which, at the end of the day, create a profitable, healthy company. That is the goal.

Small businesses are the backbone of America: Apple, Google, and other big corporations like these started from incubators in someone's garage or basement. They didn't grow overnight, but they would never have grown at all if they had been stifled by the weight of overwhelming healthcare costs. What would America look like if we didn't have the opportunity to start and grow new businesses?

Where will we be twenty years from now if we don't take control of healthcare costs today? We're going to be like Europe, where the cost of healthcare has taken up a large part of the countries' economies. Because they have socialized medicine, you don't see significant healthcare innovation coming from those countries. Major innovation is coming from the United States, where we currently have an abundance of intellectual capital to drive advancements in new technologies and thus preserving our leadership position. We are a country of over 350 million people. As a result, it is even more incumbent upon us to make sure that we maintain a healthy environment.

The need for employers to take action is clear. The following best practices checklist serves as a high-level summary of the planning activities that must take place once you have decided to make wellness a priority in your organization. Use this list to guide you as you begin implementing the ideas presented in this book:

WELLNESS STRATEGY BEST PRACTICES CHECKLIST

❏ Gain buy-in and support from senior management.

❏ Allocate budget for health and wellness programs.

❏ Craft a health and wellness vision and mission statement.

❏ Develop a communications/marketing strategy.

❏ Engage senior leaders in leading by example.

To maintain the engagement of your leadership team throughout the life of your wellness program, we recommend using WebMD Health Services' best practices:

❏ Identify the types of reports that are important to senior leaders so that they are informed and engaged and can help make meaningful decisions about the program.

❏ Interview leaders to gain important insight about their level of support, resource allocation, and commitment to actively engage.

❏ Align your health management strategy with organizational goals.

❏ Communicate frequently and consistently to all levels of leadership (senior management, midlevel, and frontline managers) who are best positioned to affect program success due to their daily interaction with employees.

❏ Invite leaders to participate in health and wellness events.

❏ Capture a CEO statement about the health management program.

❏ Identify opportunities for leaders to serve as role models and champions.

❏ Educate all management levels about the importance of the health management strategy.

❏ Make sure leadership support is visible to employees.

❏ Make appropriate program adjustments as leadership changes.

❏ Use program data to create a compelling story to share with leadership and employees.

Understand that a good wellness program takes work. You need to align yourself with someone who can help guide your employees and implement the program as a core part of what they do. As a corporate leader, you must be prepared to embrace and endorse your corporate wellness program. Be an advocate for it. Be a leader and a good example for your employees, and let them know that you are as much a part of the wellness program as they are.

Make sure that your wellness program is consistent and not an afterthought. It should be at the core of what you do every day. Too many companies start and stop their programs; they'll initiate a program, fail to follow through and then, seeing no value in it, they'll just decide that it's not working. Consistency is the key to reaping the benefits of a wellness program. By allowing employees to participate, you will, as the employer, reap those benefits of fewer sick days, enhanced productivity, and increased bottom-line profits. That's in addition to the fact that you will also be healthier, and your quality of life will improve alongside that of your employees.

The ACA has created such a demand for employers to provide benefits, that without a real culture shift, you're going to significantly increase your costs in this area. A wellness program allows you to take control again. Instead of your healthcare benefits costs controlling you and your company, you can take control of the future cost of healthcare by implementing these programs.

The key is also about understanding that the time is now: the cultivation of the ideas must happen now, the implementation is now, and the benefits will come. Evolving your company and our nation's healthcare system is going to be a long journey, so as long as you're in business, this will be an ongoing process. This will be part of your core business strategy for your employees because healthcare reform is not going away.

Likewise, employee wellness programs are evolving. By being at the forefront of these programs, you secure your company's financial future. Those companies that embrace a true wellness program that is integrated into their core business, mission statement, and lifestyle will outperform those companies that do not implement one.

You will become much more cost-efficient by having employees who are healthy. You will be able to beat your competition on pricing, and your ROI will exceed that of your competitors because you've taken the time to take action now. Ultimately, we're in business to provide a service or a product, to have engaged employees, and to grow our business—but we must understand that profitability is the fuel that makes businesses grow.

If growth is on your horizon, then now is the time to implement a wellness program.

CONTINUED PROGRESS

Progress is a basic American value that drives us to constantly improve, grow, and expand. The need to move forward, to improve upon, and to advance is in our blood. Imagine the increase in productivity and innovation that will take place when our employees and their families are healthy because wellness is the norm in organizations across the nation. Imagine the money we will save when preventable illnesses are no longer plaguing our nation's workers and driving up our healthcare premiums. Consider the ways in which we can use those saved dollars to hire more employees, create better products, and generate more revenue. I hope that this vision of a healthier, more productive America inspires you, as much as it has me, to tackle the healthcare problems in this country head on by taking initiative and committing to wellness for yourself, your family, and your organization.

If we all do our part to integrate wellness into our businesses, we can ensure that they will continue to grow and prosper despite new healthcare mandates. Together, we can generate enthusiasm and excitement about staying healthy, and in turn, staying productive and reducing the amount of money we spend, as a nation, on treating preventable diseases. Your employees and customers are counting on you to do everything you can to make your business the best it can be. If you are focused on creating a healthier workforce and reducing your healthcare premiums, then you are creating a healthier, more productive America. Commit to investing in your employees by taking the first steps toward your wellness journey. Join me in having a passion for wellness, and together we will grow and thrive.

Printed in the USA
CPSIA information can be obtained
at www.ICGtesting.com
JSHW012035140824
68134JS00033B/3069

9 781599 326146